THE TWENTIETH CENTURY THEATRE

THE
TWENTIETH CENTURY THEATRE

OBSERVATIONS ON THE CONTEMPORARY
ENGLISH AND AMERICAN STAGE

BY

WILLIAM LYON PHELPS
LAMPSON PROFESSOR OF ENGLISH LITERATURE AT YALE
MEMBER OF THE NATIONAL INSTITUTE
OF ARTS AND LETTERS

KENNIKAT PRESS, INC./PORT WASHINGTON, N. Y.

ST. PHILIPS COLLEGE LIBRARY

792
P541

THE TWENTIETH CENTURY THEATRE

Copyright 1918 by The Macmillan Company
Reissued in 1968 by Kennikat Press
Library of Congress Catalog Card No: 68-16302
Manufactured in the United States of America

ESSAY AND GENERAL LITERATURE INDEX REPRINT SERIES

To My Friend

JACK RANDALL CRAWFORD

PREFACE

THIS little book contains a discussion, with sufficient corroborative figures and specific illustrations, of some of the conditions and tendencies of the English and American stage of 1900-1918. The Modern Drama is so much greater than the Modern Theatre that we are confronted with a huge problem. We are living in the best period of play-writing since the age of Shakespeare; but how shall Americans outside of New York have an opportunity to see these new and original dramas? How can the modern theatre become a part of our national life? I have answered these two questions, but I wish I knew exactly how to bring the remedy to the patient, or to make the patient want it seriously enough to insist on having it.

Some pages of the first, second, and fifth chapters, here revised, originally appeared respectively in the *Yale Review*, October 1911, *Old Penn*, April 1916, and *The Art World*, December 1916.

W. L. P.

HURON CITY, MICHIGAN,
Tuesday, 23 *July* 1918.

CONTENTS

	PAGE
PRESENT CONDITION OF THE ANGLO-AMERICAN STAGE	1
THE DECAY OF EVIL TENDENCIES	42
THE DRAMA LEAGUE AND THE INDEPENDENT THEATRE	64
THE BIBLE AND POETRY ON THE STAGE	87
SHAKESPEARE ON THE MODERN STAGE	93
ACTORS AND ACTING	111
DRAMATIC CRITICISM	130
POSTSCRIPT	143
INDEX	145

THE TWENTIETH CENTURY THEATRE

I

PRESENT CONDITION OF THE ANGLO-AMERICAN STAGE

Pessimistic criticism always conventional — Ben Jonson and Richard Steele — recent elevation of the drama — greatest writers now dramatists — prophecies by William Sharp and Bronson Howard — literary quality of modern drama — the publication of plays — Henry Arthur Jones — Bernard Shaw on prefaces — bad conditions of the American stage — physical luxuries and spiritual necessities — the disease and the remedy — advantages of stock companies — the Artistic Theatre at Moscow — the Continent compared with America — statistics since 1900 — death of melodrama and farce — influence of the movies — the rise of Comedy — vaudeville — musical comedies and light opera.

THE fact that many sober-minded and elderly persons — who remember the days when they went fresh-eyed to the theatre — loudly condemn the modern stage, should cause no disquietude to those familiar with the history of dramatic criticism. For in almost every age it has been customary for serious folk to denounce the work done by their contemporaries, to describe it and the public taste as degenerate, and to contrast both with some mythical former time, when plays were noble and audiences discriminating. I suppose the world's high-water mark in dramatic production was about the year 1607, when Shakespeare had produced his masterpieces of tragedy and his giant comrades were in full activity. And yet in the early days of the seventeenth century, Ben Jonson, who knew the stage and the public as well as anyone, remarked not once, but repeatedly, that the condition of the drama was enough to make thoughtful men despair. In 1607, in the preface to *Volpone*, he wrote, "But it will here be hastily answered . . . that now especially in dramatick, or (as they terme it) stage-poetrie, nothing but ribaldry, profanation, blasphemy, all licence of offence to god, and man, is practis'd. I dare not denie a great part of this (and am sorry, I dare not). . . . But, that all are embarqv'd in this bold aduenture for hell, is a most vncharitable thought, and, vtter'd, a more malicious slander." Being in his own eyes one of the few living exceptions to the prevailing degradation, he declared, "I shall raise the despis'd head of poetrie againe, and stripping her out of those rotten and base rags, wherewith the Times haue adulterated her form, restore her to primitiue habit, feature, and maiesty." Again: "The encrease of which lust in liberty, together with the present trade of the Stage, in all their misc'line *Enterludes*, what learned or liberall soule doth not already abhor? where nothing but the garbage of the time is vtter'd," etc. He must have been thinking of the feeding of garbage to the bears in the bear-pit as shown by the lines (brought to my attention by Professor Rea of Earlham College) from the *Apologetical Dialogue* at the end of *Poetaster*, referring to the taste of the "multitude";

> And like the barking students of Bears-college,
> To swallow up the garbage of the time
> With greedy gullets whilst myself sit by
> Pleased, and yet tortured, with their beastly feeding.

In the Dedication to Jonson's *Catiline*, 1611, we read, "In so thick, and darke an ignorance, as now almost couers the age, . . . you dare, in these Iig-giuen times, to countenance a legitimate Poeme." Finally, in the address *To the Reader* which prefaced the quarto edition of *The Alchemist*, 1612, he said, "Thou wert neuer more fair in the way to be cosened, than in this age, in Poetrie, especially in Plays: wherein, now the concupiscence of dances and of antics so reigneth, as to run away from nature, and be afraid of her, is the only point of art that tickles the spectators. But how out of purpose, and place, do I name art?" One would think that these words were written by some sober-minded critic of a twentieth century musical comedy, rather than by Ben Jonson of his contemporaries.

Leaping a hundred years, we find Richard Steele proclaiming that intellectual interest in the drama had vanished, that all the people cared about was scenery and show, that the stage carpenter had usurped the functions of the poet. In the prologue to his play, *The Funeral*, 1701, we find

> Nature's deserted, and dramatic art,
> To dazzle now the eye, has left the heart;
> Gay lights and dresses, long extended scenes,
> Demons and angels moving in machines,
> All that can now, or please, or fright the fair,
> May be performed without a writer's care,
> And is the skill of carpenter, not player.

Without attempting any complacent whitewashing of contemporary stains, I believe that during the last thirty years the highest peaks of literature have nearly all been revealed as Drama. The foremost writers in most countries have been or are dramatists. This is such an amazing change in literary topography from the mid-nineteenth century that it forces from us observation followed by considerable reflection. Ibsen, Björnson, and Strindberg, incomparably the greatest authors in Scandinavian literature; the noblest contemporary writers in the French language, Rostand and Maeterlinck; the most powerful living man-of-letters in Italy, D'Annunzio; the leaders of contemporary literature in the German language, Hauptmann, Sudermann, Hofmannsthal, Schnitzler, Bahr; late in his career, Tolstoi devoted himself to the drama, and left posthumous plays as well; twentieth century pieces by Chekhov, Gorki, and Andreev have been acted all over the world; England's greatest living writer composed a drama of the Napoleonic wars.

During this same period there have been more good plays written in the English language than during any other succession of thirty years since the death of Shakespeare in 1616. For three centuries no generation could show such a brilliant galaxy of dramatists as Oscar Wilde, Arthur Pinero, Henry Arthur Jones, Stephen Phillips, Bernard Shaw, John Synge, W. B. Yeats, J. M. Barrie, John Galsworthy, Granville Barker. On the American side of the ocean there was no national drama until it was founded in 1890 by Clyde Fitch; since then, Augustus Thomas, William Vaughn Moody, Eugene Walter, Louis Anspacher, Jesse Williams, and others have made the dream come true. We are living in the daylight, not in the dawn.

In his *Life of Browning*, 1890, William Sharp

prophesied the coming hegemony of the Drama; and with that gift of clairvoyance that the ancients believed came with the near approach of death, Bronson Howard, a name always to be held in honour in America, uttered these eloquent and stimulating words:

> The brilliant indications shown by our younger writers for the stage who are now crowding to the front, eager, earnest, and persistent, with their eyes on the future and not the past, coming from every walk of life, from universities and all other sources of active thought, are the basis of my prophecy. It is this: In all human probability the next great revival of literature in the language will be in the theatre. The English-speaking world has been gasping for literary breath, and now we begin to feel a coming breeze. I may not live to fully enjoy it, but every man of my own age breathes the air more freely already. Let us hope that the drama of this century will yet redeem our desert of general literature. The waters of our Nile are rising.

Some reasons which partially account for the advance of the drama may be given as follows: first, the literary quality of the drama has greatly improved; second, authors all over the world who have attained success in other literary forms are turning their ambition and their talents toward the theatre; third, the custom of publishing plays has spread rapidly, and there is now actually a reading public for plays either written in or translated into English, something practically unknown outside of university courses until a few years ago. I used to hear it constantly asserted that literary skill was neither necessary nor even desirable on the stage; one must not write, one must build a play. One of our chief American dramatists, who has seen a great light since he made the remark, said that if he were not writing plays, he would not dream of writing books; he would be building bridges, or engaged in architecture. Countless stage successes have been pointed out, like *The Music Master*, for example, which are innocent of literary merit. But a change has come over the face of things. Out of a number of possible illustrations, it is worth observing that "literary" dramas like *The Blue Bird*, *The Piper*, *Fanny's First Play* and others, have been among the most successful box-office productions of the twentieth century.

Second, the fact that so many poets and novelists have become dramatists is highly significant. J. M. Barrie, John Galsworthy, Bernard Shaw, Arnold Bennett were all established novelists before they attained fame as playwrights. Stephen Phillips won renown as a poet before writing plays; the same is true of William Vaughn Moody. Hauptmann and Sudermann were respectively poet and novelist before the notable year of 1889, the beginning of modern German drama; Chekhov and Gorki had wide vogue as short-story writers before turning their attention to the stage. All this means that the ranks of the dramatists are being constantly reënforced by men-of-letters who have won distinction in some other form of literature.

Third, the publication of plays, always customary in France, did not become at all popular in England or in America in modern times until after the beginning of the twentieth century. In an article written in London in 1897, Henry James remarked: "It is one of the odd things of our actual esthetics that the more theatres multiply the less anyone reads a play — the less anyone cares, in a word, for the text of the adventure. That no one ever *does* read a play has long been a commonplace of the wisdom of booksellers." This observation, true enough when written, would now be grotesquely false. Publishers' advertisements in the twentieth century differ from those of the nineteenth in no respect more sharply than in this very thing — in fact, one might say that the printing of plays in the English language is at once the most startling and the most significant feature in the book trade of our day. The last man to hold out against the new movement was the one man who could best meet the test of print — J. M. Barrie. In 1914 he grudgingly released a few of his plays, and in 1918 he decided to publish them all.

These are golden days for the deaf — the ear is

losing importance every hour. Millions visit the movies, where the deaf are on an exact equality with those blessed or cursed with acute hearing; and the absence of repertory theatres in America is partly made up by the fact that hundreds of thousands of people *read* plays in the lamplit silence of home.

The first man in England to come out boldly and uncompromisingly for the publication of plays was that earnest and high-minded dramatist, Henry Arthur Jones. In the preface to *Saints and Sinners*, printed in 1891, he said, "In the present uncertain relations of English literature and the modern drama, an author may be excused for having some doubts as to whether the interests of either are to be served by the publication of plays whose perusal may only serve to show how sharp is the division between them. The American Copyright Bill removes these disabilities, and makes it inexcusable to yield to these doubts. If, from this time forward, a playwright does not publish within a reasonable time after the theatrical production of his piece, it will be an open confession that his work was a thing of the theatre merely, needing its garish artificial light and surroundings, and not daring to face the calm air and cold daylight of print. And further, if a custom does not now arise in England, such as prevails in France, of publishing successful plays, and if a general reading public is not gradually drawn round the drama, then it will be a sign that our stage remains in the same state of intellectual paralysis that has afflicted it all the century."

Twenty-seven years have passed since these words appeared, and the heart's desire of their author has been satisfied. It is now the custom to publish both successful and unsuccessful plays, and a general reading public has been drawn around them. Mr. Jones and Mr. Shaw follow in the wake of Dryden, not only in publishing plays, but in publishing with them significant prefaces, and indeed with Mr. Shaw the play seems no longer the thing — it is a footnote to the preface. Like Dryden and Ben Jonson, Mr. Jones appeals from the decision of the audience to the literary critics and the reading public. He believes that *Michael and His Lost Angel*, a play damned in New York, is his best work; after its failure he published it with a preface contributed by a friend, who wrote, "Some comfort in the midst of defeat may be found in the fact that the gods themselves fight vainly against prejudice and stupidity." This has the defiant ring of the author of *The New Inn;* its appeal to a higher court is interesting.

Mr. Shaw goes further; he writes prefaces defending the custom of writing prefaces, prefatory explanations of prefaces. In the preface to the volume, *Three Plays for Puritans*, he says, "The reason most dramatists do not publish their plays with prefaces is that they cannot write them, the business of intellectually conscious philosopher and skilled critic being no part of the playwright's craft. . . . I am ashamed neither of my work nor of the way it is done. I like explaining its merits to the huge majority who don't know good work from bad. . . . I write prefaces as Dryden did, and treatises as Wagner, because I can; and I would give half a dozen of Shakespeare's plays for one of the prefaces he ought to have written." So would I; indeed for such a boon I would give Mr. Shaw's complete works, and I count myself among the fervent admirers of his dramas.

In the eighteenth century, England had good theatres, great actors, and poor drama; to-day we have original plays good enough for anybody's taste, but the condition of theatrical art in America and for that matter in England needs to be altogether reformed. The one essential element — excellent modern dramas, we possess; the other side of the thing is dark, and will remain so until the only possible remedy is applied. I know exactly what the disease is, and I know exactly what remedy would cure it; but I have no idea how to bring the remedy to the patient.

THE TWENTIETH CENTURY THEATRE

Not long ago I stood at a street corner of a small New England town and marvelled at the number of automobiles that rolled by. There seemed to be almost as many Ford cars as there were inhabitants, for the streets were more crowded with these vehicles than the sidewalks were with pedestrians. I observed also that the city possessed all the advantages of modern civilisation, so far as these were concerned with physical convenience and comfort; there was every evidence of electric-lighting and steam-heating; and nobody looked hungry. Shop-windows exhibited what I assumed to be contemporary fashions in clothes — in fact, it was clear that the people of this town had everything necessary for the sustenance, protection, and adornment of the human body. It was a thoroughly contemporary American city, differing from others only in size.

Yet it had no actual theatre, no orchestra, and no art gallery. When the people wished to hear a modern play or to listen to great music, or to contemplate specimens of pictorial art, it was necessary to journey to New York.

The absence of these necessities troubled me; it troubles me still; but what troubles me more than their absence is the fact that the inhabitants are apparently not troubled at all. They think they are comfortable; they think they are modern;

they think they are civilised. "Because thou sayest, I am rich and increased with goods and have need of nothing; and knowest not that thou art wretched and miserable, and poor, and blind, and naked."

Suppose Detroit were the only town in America permitted to have motor-cars and that in order to travel in an automobile one must first of all travel to Detroit and there confine one's gasolene pilgrimages to the city limits; suppose San Francisco were the only city possessing electric lights and all others must use gas, candles, lamps, and what not; suppose Chicago were the only place where coal was used in the heating of private houses and that, owing to some fantastic monopoly — perhaps not more fantastic than some other monopolies — one must live in Chicago if one wished to have one's house properly heated in the winter. How long would Americans endure such a state of things?

Of course they would not endure it at all. Indeed, many could not endure the absence of physical luxuries while enduring easily the absence of spiritual necessities. There is a pretty reason for this which it is not necessary to demonstrate.

Dramatic art in America does not begin to touch the national life as closely or as generally as does the automobile; it has not affected, it does not affect individuals and families in their habits of thought and way of existence as the motor-car has succeeded in affecting them. Now on the Continent the contrary is true; music and dramatic art are both closer to the national life, both have a wider and a profounder influence on the daily thought of individuals and on family dinner-conversation than any vehicle for transporting the human carcass. I am not pleading for the abolishment of the automobile in America; I am suggesting that there ought to be provided in addition more opportunities for intellectual and spiritual growth.

Suppose some Briton writes a first-class play; I suppose a Briton, because he is more likely to perform such a public service than an American. Let us take a fine example — *What Every Woman Knows*, by J. M. Barrie. This is a drama full of thought, full of action, full of charm — a great play. Every city and town in the United States ought to have the opportunity of seeing and hearing it, and it would be an enormous gain if we could all see and hear it at the same time. What are the terms by which an American may be permitted to witness it at all? It is produced at one theatre in one town by one company. The management hopes that it will run there at least a year. During that year if any person in Cleveland or Buffalo or St. Louis or

THE TWENTIETH CENTURY THEATRE

Chicago or Salt Lake City happens to want to hear this drama performed, he must journey to New York, and succeed in the endeavour to buy a seat at the particular building where it is being produced. After the lapse of a year, or perhaps two or three years, it may be taken on the road, and it may or may not come within the range of the people living in the towns I have mentioned. Americans endure this situation in dramatic art without a protest; whereas if the case in question were some physical luxury, they would not endure it for a moment.

In some European countries, when a new play is produced in one of the large cities and the thing is successful, within a week every other city and many of the small towns are enjoying the same piece. This means that everybody in the country is talking about the same play at the same time — discussing it, arguing about it, reading criticisms of it in the local papers. The new play is an educational force; it is really a part of the national life. Europeans have often the same curiosity in dramatic art that we have in mechanical inventions, devices to lower expenses and increase profits, or a new system of dieting. A significant play in Europe is discussed with something of the same general eagerness that Americans talked about the book *Eat and Grow Thin*. It is a national sensation.

Now Americans by nature are not one whit more

materialistic than Europeans. We simply are not informed as to what ought to be the condition of dramatic art. I am certain that if we had the opportunity we should take advantage of it. There is an immense amount of intellectual and spiritual hunger in America. The so-called "practical" and shrewd theatre-managers who are the shepherds of our souls have a lower opinion of our intelligence than the facts warrant. Over and over again they decline to give us good music and good drama, because they are so cocksure we do not want it. When John Galsworthy's new play *Justice* was brought to America it was offered in turn to a succession of dramatic managers, who contemptuously rejected it. "The American people will never stand for that high-brow stuff." Finally one person was found who was willing to risk the venture. To the amazement of the "practical" men the play turned out to be an enormous financial success; night after night the house was crowded.

That the American people desire only trashy plays and frothy music is a fallacy almost impossible to uproot from the managerial mind. In the midst of the hot summer of 1916 somebody in New York had the amazing audacity to hire a hall and announce a concert made up exclusively of classical compositions. The thermometer reached about one hundred degrees that evening, yet the vast hall was packed and jammed with a wildly enthusiastic audience. Perhaps it is a mistake to suppose, first, that Americans do not want the best in art, and second, that their minds hibernate in heat. I remember, some years ago, when a thoroughly intellectual dramatic performance was given at a New York theatre, the interest was so great that hundreds could not get admission; and the next day the New York *Sun*, devoting a column to the phenomenon, suggested to theatrical managers that merely as a matter of business it might be well to consider the number of "high-brows" in New York — that perhaps it was not always necessary to scale every production down to a level of insipidity.

It is evident that two things are necessary before we shall have anything like a diffusion of dramatic art in America. *There must be a stock company in every city, and every company must have the right to produce new plays.* If I were a playwright I had rather make a small profit from each of many performances on a single night than a large profit from one. Although the stock company has never had a fair trial on a universal scale in America, the few illustrations of it that we have had are so strikingly superior to the star system that the case for dramatic art is already proven. In the eighties

THE TWENTIETH CENTURY THEATRE

Augustin Daly's company presented both Shakespearean and contemporary dramas in a manner that fills one's memory with vivid delight; in the nineties Daniel Frohman's Lyceum company was incomparably the finest example of dramatic art in America; one was certain of a good production every time. I regard Daniel Frohman as one of our most high-minded and sincere theatrical managers. I believe he has been actuated always by lofty motives, for he has lent dignity to every undertaking associated with his name. I suspect that the period when he was in control of the old Lyceum Theatre represents some of the happiest years of his life.

American stock companies, however, are not merely memories. During the season of 1915-1916 Miss Grace George — a charming and accomplished actress — established a stock company in New York that immediately took its place at the head of metropolitan theatres. Their presentation of Bernard Shaw's *Major Barbara* was so near impeccability that it is no exaggeration to call it absolutely satisfactory. This was one of the four great events of the season; the other three being Hauptmann's *Weavers* (in English), Galsworthy's *Justice*, and the only original American play of any importance: *The Unchastened Woman* by Louis K. Anspacher. It will be observed that the proportion of excellent native productions is one in four; if this can be kept up for ten years, I shall be satisfied. America is so far behind Europe in dramatic art that if we can write one-quarter of the plays really worth hearing, we shall be doing well. Mr. Anspacher's comedy would be a credit to any dramatist in the world.

The greatest day in the history of the American stage was the fifteenth of December, 1908, the laying of the corner-stone of the New Theatre. As an American I am and always shall be unspeakably grateful to the Founders. They showed a generosity and a courage in this undertaking representative of the highest and purest patriotism. One would have thought that such a vast enterprise would have been "news"; would have been worthy of the ablest editorial discussion. Yet on the dawn of that historic day not one notice of the event did I find in any New York newspaper; and although the afternoon's exercises were graced by the presence of the Mayor, President Finley, Augustus Thomas, John Bigelow, Daniel Frohman, and Geraldine Farrar, not one editorial could I discover in the big metropolitan journals the next morning. The closeness of dramatic art in America to the national life may be estimated by this uniform silence.

I am well aware that the New Theatre turned out

to be a financial failure, and from the common point of view, no failure can be worse than that. But just as some financial successes do not deeply benefit the public, so there may be financial failures that leave in their wake permanent blessings. During the two years in which the New Theatre existed America had the greatest stock company it ever possessed; a company really on a par with the *Comédie Française*. It was a company that could and did produce contemporary plays so totally unlike as *Sister Béatrice* and *Don*, and produce both in a manner that left nothing to be desired. It was a company that — after the ghastly failure of *Antony and Cleopatra* — gave the most thrilling performances of Shakespeare that have ever adorned our stage. It was a company that raised the whole level of dramatic art in America; that has made Americans more dissatisfied with cheap and sloppy acting than they used to be; that has left in the minds of many Americans a determination never to be satisfied until we have something like it again. No wonder that many individuals who had invested in theatrical management purely as a speculative business joined in a wolfish attack on this enterprise! Their sure business instinct told them of a mortal peril; they had little difficulty in recognising a powerful foe. For if Americans should once become accustomed to a high standard of company-acting, as Parisians are, what would become of the tenth-rate stars backed by the speculators?

But it is not merely in a general way that the New Theatre left its impression. Four distinct and specific results — all of great value — followed more or less directly from its influence. Mr. Winthrop Ames founded the Little Theatre; and while he has not always been fortunate in his pieces, the performances under his direction are better than those given in most New York theatres, and the emphasis is all on team-play. Mr. Granville Barker was induced to come to New York, and present under his own training and direction *Androcles and the Lion*, *The Man Who Married a Dumb Wife*, *The Doctor's Dilemma*, and *Midsummer-Night's Dream*. Intelligent people may fairly differ as to the value of all of Mr. Barker's ideas; the blessed thing is that *he has ideas*, a scarce article in the American theatre. For my part I think the excellence of the acting in *The Doctor's Dilemma* was a revelation, and the stage setting of *The Dumb Wife* exceedingly beautiful. Third, Miss Grace George was emboldened to establish a stock company in New York that should present high-class dramas in a manner worthy of the best European traditions; and fourthly, Mr. Louis Calvert, literally one of the best actors in the world

— who made a profound impression in every rôle that he played in the New Theatre — has determined to make America his home. In Grace George's company he shone with real distinction in *Major Barbara*, and in conjunction with John Corbin — also connected with the New Theatre — he produced in the spring of 1916 *The Tempest*, the most memorable Shakespearean event in a great Shakespearean year. I trace all four of these immense advances in dramatic art directly to the splendid experiment of the New Theatre. I hope the founders do not feel that their efforts were wholly in vain.

When I say that the only chance for American dramatic art lies in the general adoption of the stock company and the universal right to produce new plays, I have in mind, of course, real stock companies conducted on the European plan. Meanwhile in many cities we have something that is worthy of high praise, for it is a step — only a step — in the right direction. This is the leasing of some theatre by a manager, who hires a stock company at rather low salaries and produces each week a once-famous play; with so small a price for seats that practically everybody can afford to attend occasionally. An excellent illustration of this system may be found in the city of New Haven, where Mr. Sylvester Poli bought the Hyperion Theatre, and now, with a fairly good company, gives representative plays with a weekly change of bill. The programme is sufficiently varied to be interesting; and Mr. Poli is a benefactor in presenting such a play as Augustus Thomas's masterpiece, *The Witching Hour*, one of the best of all original American dramas. This enterprise has been enormously successful; the theatre is packed at every performance; hundreds buy a weekly subscription ticket, retaining the same seats for the season; and it would be difficult to over-estimate the amount of pleasure that has been added to the lives of many persons, who look forward to the subscription day with unfeigned delight. Apart from the pleasure of witnessing farces, comedies, and melodramas, this theatre acts as a kind of laboratory for students of the drama; for by specimens it really represents the history of the American stage during the last twenty years and affords in some cases the opportunity for young playwrights to produce an original piece.

With all its advantages it is not, however, the kind of stock company I have in mind. This remark would be absurdly obvious were it not that those who defend the star system always assume that "stock" means just this and nothing more. Mr. Poli's company is forced to give twelve performances a week; the same actors appear in every production and the leading actors always take the leading rôles. This entails a prodigious amount of work for rehearsals in addition to the time spent on production: no one has any rest, and I wonder when the actors find time to sleep.

In a high-class stock company there are no stars; he who takes a leading rôle one night does not appear at all the next night, and on the third night may have an infinitesimally small part. The members of the company have time to study, to rest, to visit other theatres, to live a normal life. Best of all, they are enabled to be really citizens of the town where the company plays, to secure a permanent home, send their children to the public schools, become members of society, with all the happiness and all the responsibility thereof. Actors and actresses by nature are no worse than other people; what would happen to many of our so-called respectable citizens if they were in a different town every night, with no responsibilities and with nothing to do except from seven to eleven in the evening? A commercial traveler told me he faced more temptations in a week than I face in a year, and I believe him. In Europe the actors and actresses are as welcome in society as the college professors; one actor in 1904 told me he had just signed a contract that secured him a place in the local theatre until 1919! During all these years he has a home with his wife and children; he has an opportunity to advance in art by constantly studying new and different rôles. I could not help comparing his case with that of an American college graduate I met in Detroit, who was "on the road" in *Brewster's Millions* and had acted the same minor rôle in this drama for three years.

Even as the New Theatre was the most important dramatic event in America in the twentieth century, so Miss Horniman's Manchester Repertory Theatre, founded in 1908, has done an immense service for the cause of good drama in England. Six years ago, being in London at the height of the dramatic season, it seemed to me a significant fact that Miss Horniman's company, from the provinces, gave in an out-of-the-way building, and at considerably smaller admission-prices, examples of good plays well acted that surpassed nearly everything at the regular theatres. There I saw Galsworthy's *Silver Box*, Arnold Bennett's *What the Public Wants*, and other excellent contemporary pieces adequately produced. Miss Horniman's work with the Abbey Theatre, and her ten fruitful years with the Manchester company, have made her one of the most important leaders in modern theatrical history. There is simply no comparison between the results she has achieved and those coming from the conventional star system, long run, and play-monopoly.

THE TWENTIETH CENTURY THEATRE

If half of what I hear about it be true, the Artistic Theatre at Moscow under the directorship of Mr. Stanislavski has the finest stock company in the world. For seven years there was an annual deficit; then up to the Great War, it more than paid its expenses. The Director regards team-play in his company as essential as we know it to be in football; no one is allowed to monopolise the spotlight. If some famous star wishes to become a member of the company, he is admitted only on condition that he consent not to appear in public for one year, for it takes that length of time to get the star-poison out of his system. He rehearses with the company, and becomes acquainted with them and with their methods. After Chekhov's great play *The Cherry Orchard* failed in Petrograd, it was produced in 1904 at the Artistic Theatre in Moscow with such overwhelming success that it is still one of the most called-for pieces. Perhaps the highest compliment this company received was when Maeterlinck, after writing *The Blue Bird*, had it translated from French into Russian, and requested that the first night of its performance should be at the Artistic Theatre in Moscow. From that building it spread all over Europe, and became one of the favourite plays of the New Theatre in New York.

In Stockholm there are more theatres in propor-

THE TWENTIETH CENTURY THEATRE

tion to the population than in any other city in the world; and in a week, one may hear classic and modern plays, native and foreign.

In six successive days in Paris, I heard performed two tragedies by Racine, one tragedy by Victor Hugo, one comedy by Regnard, one comedy by Goldoni, one drama by Dumas, one comedy by Augier, one contemporary piece by Brieux, and two comedies by Molière! At one of the frequent classic matineés, the best seats in the house were sold for fifty cents, a distinguished literary man gave a short lecture preliminary to the representation, and the theatre was packed with high school boys and girls, nearly all of whom had a copy of the text in their hands, and made notes on the margin. Think of the educational value of such an institution, if we could combine it with school education in our country! If the teacher could say to the pupils, "This week we are studying *Twelfth Night;* on Thursday afternoon the local stock company will give a performance of this play. I advise you all to attend, and on Friday we shall discuss it in the class."

Outside of New York City — the only town where the drama can be studied in America — the conditions of theatrical art seem to need improvement. I remember not so very long ago reading at the head of the dramatic column in a newspaper published in Massachusetts:

THE TWENTIETH CENTURY THEATRE

CHOICE WEEK IN HOLYOKE

Holyoke Opera House to Hear Some of Best Independent Productions — Attractions of the Week

HOLYOKE OPERA HOUSE

Monday, Tuesday, and Wednesday evenings, — matinées daily —
Washington Society Girls' Extravaganza Company

EMPIRE THEATRE

Monday, Tuesday, and Wednesday evenings —
The Two Johns
Thursday, Friday, and Saturday evenings, — matinées daily —
High Rollers Extravaganza Company

Now if this is a choice week in Holyoke, what do you suppose is the local conception of an *average* sennight?

But let us leave the smaller places, and travel westward. I will give specimen days all within the last few years. In Utica, I observed there was to be one vaudeville and one burlesque; in Syracuse, *The Globe Trotters*, and two vaudevilles; in the splendid city of Cleveland, only one play, with the significant title, *Nobody Home;* and in Detroit, a city that prides itself on its prodigious growth, I found in the autumn the following legend at the head of theatrical news:

THE TWENTIETH CENTURY THEATRE

REGULAR SEASON IS USHERED IN

With one of the regular theatres throwing its doors open to-morrow night, and two others, including a newcomer, announcing their initial attractions, the local theatrical season can be said to be fairly with us. A musical comedy new to Detroit, a farce comedy pleasantly remembered, because of a previous presentation, a series of traveltalks and vaudeville of a varied nature are noted in the following list:

DETROIT — "Dew Drop Inn."
GARRICK — Lyman Howe's Traveltalks.
LYCEUM — "Nearly Married."
TEMPLE — Conroy and LeMaitre.
ORPHEUM — Gus Hornbrook's Wild West Show.
MILES — "The Unfair Sex."
GAYETY — Sam Howe's Big Show.
CADILLAC — "The Lady Buccaneers."

I heard no protest from anyone in Detroit, but I do not believe that everybody in that fine city was really satisfied with the "opening" of the regular season.

Let us proceed to Chicago:

THE WEEK'S PLAYBILLS

CORT — "Up Stairs and Down," a social satire by Mr. and Mrs. Hatton, with Fred Tiden, Mary Servoss, Frances Ring, Leo Carillo, Ethel Stanard, Orlando Daly, and others. To-night.

LA SALLE — "Oh, Boy!"

THE TWENTIETH CENTURY THEATRE

Garrick — "You're in Love."

Olympic — Last week of Fiske O'Hara in "The Man from Wicklow." Next Sunday — "Parlor, Bedroom, and Bath."

Palace — Final week of "The Show of Wonders."

Grand — Nearing the end of "Turn to the Right."

Illinois — William Courtenay and Thomas A. Wise in "Pals First," a nice crook play.

Powers' — "Oh, So Happy!" a musical comedy.

Majestic — Vaudeville, including Nan Halperin, Leona Le Mar, Collins and Hart, Billie Montgomery, and George Perry, the Pearl of Hawaii, and others.

Wilson Avenue — "Seven Keys to Baldpate."

Colonial — Vaudeville, with "The Smart Shop."

Rialto — Vaudeville, with Richard the Great, a trained monkey.

McVicker's — Vaudeville, with "The Fascinating Flirts."

National — "The Marriage Question."

Going south to one of the most progressive towns in America, Birmingham, Alabama, I discovered the following theatrical refreshment:

AT THE THEATRES

Lyric — Vaudeville. Matinée at 3 o'clock. Night performances at 7:30 and 9 o'clock.

Bijou — Dramatic success, "A Little Girl in a Big City." Matinée at 2:30. Night performance at 8:30.

Majestic — Musical comedy, "Honeymoon Girls," and pictures.

THE TWENTIETH CENTURY THEATRE

Ah, but in saying that New York was the only town where it is possible to study the drama, have I not made one fatal omission? Have I not forgotten Boston? I remember reading in a European novel that Boston is "the centre of American intelligence." It is certainly true that the opportunities to hear music and to regard pictures are abundant and adequate; how about the drama?

NEXT WEEK

BOSTON OPERA HOUSE — Andrew Mack in "Molly Dear," first time.

COPLEY — "The Man Who Stayed at Home."

COLONIAL — "Ziegfeld Follies" 1917.

GLOBE — "The Wolf."

HOLLIS STREET — Ruth Chatterton in "Come Out of the Kitchen."

MAJESTIC — "Seven Days' Leave."

PARK SQUARE — "Captain Kidd, Jr.," first time.

PLYMOUTH — "Oh, Boy."

SHUBERT — "The Passing Show of 1917."

TREMONT — "Turn to the Right."

WILBUR — "Love o' Mike," with George Hassell.

B. F. KEITH'S — Conroy and La Maire, etc.

ORPHEUM — Raymond and Caverly, etc.

GAYETY — "The Behman Show."

CASINO — The New Bon Ton Girls.

HOWARD — The Innocent Maids Co.

BOSTON — Jane Cowl in "The Spreading Dawn," etc.

PARK — Mme. Petrova in "The Spreading Dawn," etc.

GORDON'S OLYMPIA — Douglas Fairbanks in "The Man from Painted Post," etc.

SCOLLAY SQUARE OLYMPIA — Charlie Chaplin in "The Adventure," etc.

FENWAY — George Walsh in "The Yankee Way," etc.

EXETER STREET — Jack Pickford and Louise Huff in "The Ghost House," etc.

BOWDOIN SQUARE — "The Spy," with Dustin Farnum, etc.

MODERN — Marguerite Clark in "Bab's Burglar," etc.

LANCASTER — George Walsh in "The Yankee Way," etc.

ST. JAMES — Frescott, etc.

In New York, while there are no such opportunities to hear ancient and contemporary drama as there are in Continental cities, we find the only place in America where new plays may be observed, and the standard of excellence is much higher than it was twenty years ago. American taste in general may be estimated by the following table, which shows the percentage for November, 1899, in the theatres of the following representative cities: New York, Boston, Philadelphia, Chicago, Cleveland, St. Louis, Baltimore, and Washington:

Tragedy and Melodrama	34
Comedy	23
Farce	12
Light Opera	10
Grand Opera	6
Vaudeville, Burlesque, etc.	15

THE TWENTIETH CENTURY THEATRE

It must be remembered that my classification is somewhat arbitrary, and that critics would never be unanimous in designating certain plays as comedies, others as farces, others as melodramas. The New York *Tribune*, the only newspaper that attempts any classification in its weekly review, would not put on every play the same label as mine. Yet on the majority we should agree. It is clear that *Hamlet* is a tragedy, *The Thirteenth Chair* a melodrama, *A Kiss for Cinderella* a comedy, and *Excuse Me* a farce. Under the title *Light Opera* I am forced to include the so-called musical comedies, and under vaudeville all variety entertainments and music-hall shows.

Between the first of October and the first of May on any week-day night in New York the theatregoer has his choice among about forty performances. The table on the following page summarises at a glance the metropolitan theatres during the last eighteen years.

Several interesting conclusions may be drawn from this table. In the early years of the century the dying melodrama had a false semblance of life. This was caused, I think, by the rage for pseudo-historical romances in prose fiction, many of which were transferred to the stage, as we shall see later, when we consider the dramatised novel. But the public sense of humour eventually got the best

THE TWENTIETH CENTURY THEATRE

	5 Mar. 1900	2 Mar. 1901	15 Jan. 1902	9 Mar. 1903	4 Mar. 1904	9 Feb. 1905	1 Mar. 1906	14 Mar. 1907	17 Dec. 1908	23 Feb. 1909	4 Mar. 1910	14 Apr. 1911	18 Dec. 1912	12 Mar. 1913	14 Dec. 1914	17 Nov. 1915	7 Feb. 1916	9 Feb. 1917	28 Jan. 1918
Tragedy	3	0	3	3	1	1	1	3	0	1	0	0	1	0	0	0	2	0	0
Melodrama	7	7	9	8	5	9	9	8	5	7	3	5	4	5	4	3	2	3	3
Comedy	6	9	7	6	10	9	9	11	11	10	15	12	15	18	16	17	18	22	22
Farce	3	5	4	1	4	8	5	7	7	4	4	4	4	4	3	2	4	2	2
Light opera	3	2	4	11	7	7	4	6	6	6	7	7	5	7	4	7	6	7	9
Grand opera	1	1	1	1	1	1	0	0	2	0	3	1	2	1	1	1	1	2	2
Vaudeville	12	8	7	11	11	12	14	9	8	11	11	9	11	11	10	5	7	7	5
Total	35	32	35	41	39	47	42	44	39	39	43	38	42	46	38	35	40	43	43

both of the dramatised romance and stage melodrama, especially among metropolitan audiences, as was shown by the fact that the elaborate revival in the spring of 1911 of *The Lights of London* was greeted by New York spectators with unrestrained guffaws and ironical applause. Its place was taken by a hybrid called melodramatic farce or farcical melodrama, of which *Officer 666* is a good specimen. But the knock-out blow to both pure melodrama and pure farce was given by the moving pictures, for a glance at the table will show that each of these forms went down and out at approximately the same time. And the reason is clear; why should one pay two dollars to see *No Wedding Bells for Her* when one can see it in the movies for a dime? Why should one pay two dollars to see a clown hit a United States Senator in the face with a wedge of custard pie, when one can see Charlie Chaplin do it for ten cents?

Indeed the movies have not only had an extinguishing effect on melodrama and farce, they have severely wounded music hall shows, and now we often see the vaudeville unite itself with the pictures.

The movie habit is a bad habit. I think I see its effect on many young people to-day, who are more loose-lipped than formerly. In conversation, they seem to endeavour to turn their mouths inside out, and I ascribe this unpleasant fashion to the movie habit — they have been watching the silent actors and actresses "registering" emotion.

> Kind gentlemen, your pains are registered
> Where every day I turn the leaf to read them.

But the movie habit is not the fault of the movies, but of the people who attend too frequently — and even so it is better than the saloon habit, which it has done much to replace. The movies have had this excellent effect on the legitimate theatre. They have jacked it up. It is vain for the theatre to contend with the movies by the weapons of mere entertainment; there the movies make a stronger appeal, and at one-twentieth the price. No, if the theatre is to hold any place at all, it must furnish something in addition to mere entertainment; it must have ideas, cerebration, clever or powerful dialogue. The movies, then, have forced the theatre to a higher plane of art, and I am grateful for the service rendered.

The rise of Comedy, as exhibited in the table, is highly significant. It is the most encouraging single fact in the twentieth century theatre. It should always lead, as it does now in New York, other forms of dramatic art, for Comedy is the reflection and the interpretation of life. That way

THE TWENTIETH CENTURY THEATRE

lies the hope of the theatre. Would that the modern comedy could imitate the movies in giving every town in the country an opportunity to see the same play at the same time! The effect of such moving pictures as *The Birth of a Nation* and *Les Misérables* is prodigiously heightened by the fact that the whole country is seeing them during the same season. San Francisco, Chicago, New Orleans, and New York eagerly discuss the same moving picture. As this consummation for modern comedy is the one above all others devoutly to be wished, it is pleasant to record the one and only attempt at realisation that I know. When Mr. Robert Housum, the author of the best original American comedy during the autumn of 1917 — I mean *The Gipsy Trail* — mounted it in New York under the skilful direction of Arthur Hopkins, it was also produced during the same week in Chicago; so that for the first time in human history, two American cities were beholding a new comedy at the same moment.

We have to a large extent got rid of cheap melodrama and cheap farce — both excellent forms of entertainment, if taken in moderation, but not conducive to theatrical art. Vaudeville no longer outranks Comedy as it did in the early years of the century. It will never die, and it ought not to. It is an excellent form of entertainment.

THE TWENTIETH CENTURY THEATRE

The ancient soprano — a sentimental ruin — the exotic gymnasts with their family tree — the trained cats — the juggler who tosses a silver dollar in the air and catches it in his eye — these are often delightful to witness, and the blessed thing about the whole show is this: that if any feature is overpoweringly dull or inane, and some are both — we know that it cannot last long. It must give way to something better. Occasionally too, the vaudeville contains some exhibition of true art. I shall never forget the two birdmen, with their ornithological love-duet dialogue, that I saw at the Hippodrome a year ago. For that matter, Charles Dillingham's Hippodrome is a public benefaction.

There is no doubt that the vaudeville-movie combination has an immense hold on the popular heart, although outside of New York the vaudeville portion seems to me almost incredibly inane, an insult to the intelligence of humanity. I happened to be for an hour in a New England city, during the month of October, 1917, because of bad train connections. I therefore paid my dime and entered a huge auditorium. The day was Monday, the hour was three, and the weather ideally beautiful. Every seat in the huge room and galleries was occupied, and I was one of many forced to stand. I did not stand long, for the part of the show that

THE TWENTIETH CENTURY THEATRE

I witnessed — two persons trying to be funny — filled me with the thickest gloom. What impressed me was the fact that so many hundreds of able-bodied men and women, in the middle of a beautiful Monday afternoon, had nothing better to occupy their attention than this.

On the Continent, good vaudeville flourishes side by side with legitimate drama, and the two are never confused in the public mind. American travellers carry away pleasant memories of the music halls, where the parquet floor is covered with tables, and a good-natured crowd eat, drink, and smoke while the performance makes its devious, disconnected, and merry march. But the theatres know well enough that if they are to maintain their popularity against this hydra-headed rival, they must make a quite different appeal. They must supply the audiences not only with an interesting spectacle, but with food for actual mental fletcherising; their plays must have, not necessarily instruction, but ideas. In Europe the vaudeville has helped the theatre as the movies have helped it in America.

The sudden rise of musical comedy in 1903 is a curious fact and the practical disappearance of comic opera on the American stage is a public misfortune. By comic opera I mean of course the works of Gilbert and Sullivan, and such light masterpieces as *Erminie, Robin Hood*, and *The Serenade*. These passed away with the dying century; a glance at the table shows how few were the "musical shows" in 1900, 1901, and 1902. Then appeared an upstart crow, beautified with the feathers of the old light opera and resembling it as the song of the crow resembles that of the nightingale. This dramatic freak was called "musical comedy," a curiously infelicitous appellation, as it usually lacked both music and humour. Within the last two years, indeed, the managers are more frank, for this kind of entertainment is now frequently advertised as "Girl and music show." Suddenly it reached a climax in 1903, and like ping-pong, was all the rage; then it began to droop, and might have faded altogether were it not for the war. We are sharing in this respect the experience of England, for it is believed that both soldiers and civilians, as a reaction and refuge from the general sorrow, demand something "snappy." Everyone to his taste; for my part I find in time of war such a masterpiece as J. M. Barrie's *The Old Lady Shows Her Medals* more restorative than vulgar inanity. Is it not only better, but more refreshing, to devote what time we have free from war-work to great books, great music, great plays rather than to jarring idiocies? At a splendid performance of the Ninth Symphony in New York in

1918, it was a pleasure to me to see so many soldiers in the audience. It all depends, of course, on what you call depressing. To me a superb tragedy adequately acted is not depressing; it is nobly exhilarating. There is nothing so depressing as stupidity. The last time I went to a musical comedy I went away steeped in gloom. I felt as if a misfortune had happened to me, and it had.

Perhaps the only way to destroy musical comedy is to revive comic opera. There are thousands of theatre-goers hungry for it. When *The Mikado* was revived in New York in 1910, at the end of the theatrical season, the public interest was prodigious; it had been the intention to give only a few performances, but the demand was so keen and constant that *The Mikado* ran its triumphant course deep into the sultry summer. The same success greeted *Pinafore* in 1911. In 1918, Victor Herbert, who is more capable than any one else in America of writing light opera, produced *Eileen;* a piece full of lovely melodies, real humour and charm. After gazing for many years at the American stage — bare, ruined choirs, where late the sweet bird sang — *Eileen* was as welcome as a friendly face in a distant desert.

II

THE DECAY OF EVIL TENDENCIES

Some evil tendencies checked — the lust for scenery — later improvements — Granville Barker — Gordon Craig — the theatrical trust — rise of prices for theatre seats — speculators — F. Ziegfeld, Jr. — dramatisation of popular novels — its effect on dramatic art — its impulse to melodrama — prize-fighters on the stage — growth of original American comedy — the exportation of American plays — proper hour for beginning performances — concentration.

MUSICAL comedy is just now the most dangerous foe of dramatic art in both England and America; but I cannot believe that it has any element of permanence, and I think I shall outlive it. It is encouraging to remember that at the beginning of the twentieth century there were a number of evil tendencies seriously threatening the theatre which died a natural death. One of these was the rivalry among producers to satisfy and to stimulate the lust of the eye. In 1902 a spectator of *The Darling of the Gods* declared that he saw more scenery in five minutes than Shakespeare saw in his whole life. Just as rival railways, whose limited trains made the same time and charged the same price, felt compelled to compete in the luxury of dining and observation cars, so various theatres began to compete in gorgeous spectacular effects. A profusion of splendid scenery not only fails to help the imagination, it debases it. The love of mere scenic effect has in reality no rational connexion with true drama. It bears about the same relation to legitimate drama as a kaleidoscope bears to a telescope. The Puritans worshipped God in a cold, bare rectangular room, not because they lacked imagination, but because their imagination was so boldly and pictorially vivid, that in this barren space they saw the heavens opened, and the revelation of celestial glory. Whatever Elizabethan audiences lacked, they did not lack imagination. It would be foolish to insist on an empty stage; but I had rather have that than one stuffed with gaudy scenery. This sudden rage for bogus splendour died away; its place has been taken with adequate stage settings.

Most present-day theatre-goers can remember when a living-room on the stage had no ceiling, and when the doors — covered along the edge with dirty marks left there by scene-shifters — swung back and forth after an exit like the pendulum of a clock running down. How seldom did we see on the stage a practicable door, that shut with a real click! After the spasm for splendour passed, adequate scenery took its place. Now we have ceilings, windows, and doors that do not distract attention from the play by violating verisimilitude; and it may be that some day we shall behold an open-air scene where the sky has no wrinkles. Scenic effects, like clothes, should be unobtrusive.

And, while dressing the stage so that the scenery shall be subordinate to the drama and at the same time shall assist in interpreting it, it is quite possible to have exquisite beauty without a suggestion of tawdry ornamentation. Granville Barker's famous visit to New York stimulated the American theatre in many directions, all good. His staging of the second act of *The Doctor's Dilemma* was an ideal illustration of what I mean by adequate scenery full of beauty; and no one who saw *The Man who Married a Dumb Wife* will ever forget the setting for that comedy. It was a work of flawless art, and in my memory will be a joy forever.

In all that has to do with the presentation of plays, revolutionary and interesting ideas have been originated by Gordon Craig. He thoroughly mastered the old technique before developing something different. His first appearance as an actor was in 1889, at the Lyceum Theatre in London, under the direction of Henry Irving. After eight years of practical histrionic experience, he began the study of the art of the theatre, and his school in Florence attracted the attention of the world. It is not necessary to support all of his schemes, some of which seem like vagaries, to record gratitude to him for his aims. John Cournos, in an article in *Poetry and Drama*, September, 1913, sums up in one paragraph the essence of Mr. Craig's philosophy. "The function of the theatre, as he comprehends it, is not to present the superficial semblances of life, but the soul of life; not Naturalism, but suggestion; not representation, but interpretation; not dialogue, but action; not scenery, but atmosphere; not ideas, but visions."

Whether Mr. Craig's schemes should be definitely adopted or not, is beside the point; the point is that his ideas are bound to elevate both the stage and the audience.

In order to show how we have progressed away from mere indiscriminate stage splendour since the year 1900, I will quote a few lines from a thoughtful review of the decline of the theatre written by Mr. A. C. Wheeler in *Harper's Weekly* at the beginning of the twentieth century.

> Goethe one day, after witnessing a poor play — it was probably one of Kotzebue's — went home and set down these words: "The ordinary man is content to see something going on."
>
> That can hardly be said now of the ordinary man at the

theatre. He must see a great many things going on simultaneously, and there is some excuse for it in the fact that a great many more things *are* going on at the end than were going on at the beginning of the century.

Some recognition of that fact is necessary in appraising the theatre and in attempting to measure the progress of the amusement-going man through the hundred years. For it is on the side of his apprehensions that the theatrical appeal is apparent, and its appeals to-day are more various and kinetoscopic than ever before. There is so much going on that calls upon his cognitions without disturbing his reflection that his visual faculty has grown out of all proportion to his other senses. The theatre, instead of purging and disciplining his eye, has simply pampered and prostituted it. He does not hear as well and as patiently as he did one hundred years ago. The playhouse, which from Garrick's time insisted on being a mirror, has quadrupled the facets on its reflecting surface, and to the eye of our time it is the most vivid, the most alluring, and the most multiform of every appeal made to the sense.

To-day we hear comparatively little about the Theatrical Trust — a subject hotly discussed in and out of the courts at the beginning of the century. Some of its worst evils have disappeared. The organisation of the theatres into an iron-clad trust was bad chiefly because — whatever may be the situation in purely commercial activities — in art there is one principle absolutely essential — Liberty. The trust then interfered with the liberty of the playwright, the actor, and the local

THE TWENTIETH CENTURY THEATRE

manager. It was as though a sculptor should decide to make a statue of Mars, only to discover that a rich merchant had bought up all the marble — he must make statues dictated by the art-ignorant magnate, or make no statues at all. There is more liberty now than there was eighteen years ago, and the good qualities of organisation have developed more than the bad.

During the last ten years the prices of nearly everything wanted by human beings have gone up with appalling velocity. Nearly everything — not everything. It is notable that while we have to pay more for almost every necessary or desirable object on earth than we did ten years ago, the price of a theatre-ticket remains the same. The upward tendency received a check, and the reasons for it are interesting. When I was an undergraduate in New Haven, the best seats in the theatre ordinarily cost one dollar; when Edwin Booth appeared, they rose to a dollar and a half. In a few years, the standard price for any play became a dollar and a half; and before the end of the nineteenth century, it rose to two dollars. Then when Henry Irving or Sarah Bernhardt arrived, they were able to charge three dollars. Beerbohm Tree — a poor actor — made his first appearance in New York as Hamlet; I still regret the three dollars I was forced to pay. I once gave — God forgive me for it! — five dollars to see an all-star cast in *The Rivals*. Such incidents made me firmly believe that by 1918 the fixed price for an ordinary theatrical entertainment would be three or four dollars. I was mistaken. The price is what it was twenty years ago — two dollars — and in many cases has relapsed to a dollar and a half. If theatre-seats had climbed like other commodities, we should now be paying five or six dollars a chair. Indeed, after America's entrance into the war, a number of managers attempted to force the price to two dollars and a half. They were quickly obliged to haul in their horns.

All speculation in theatre-seats is a bad thing; there should be one standard price and seats should be obtainable only at the box-office, either by the purchaser orally, or by a bank cheque through the post. As it is now, those who go to the box office or send a cheque thither, even for a performance two weeks in advance, often receive the worst seats in the house. This should be reformed altogether.

A day or two after I had written the above paragraph, I was pleased to see in a New York newspaper a long letter from F. Ziegfeld, Jr., announcing that the New Amsterdam Theatre would sell seats only at the box office. While his particular show has no interest for me, I commend heartily his courage in fighting the speculators and the hotels. His position is correct, and I hope he will succeed not only in his own theatre, but that his example will be followed by others. Here follows a portion of his admirable statement, which appeared in the early summer of 1918:

Three weeks and five days have passed since I inaugurated my fight against ticket profiteering, and the gross takings of the *Follies* for that period are $103,732, the government receiving approximately $9430 for that period. It is with regret that in an article printed in one of the morning papers interviews with other managers showed them lukewarm in their attitude and remarks regarding the abolishing in New York of ticket profiteering. Their attitude evidently was the fear that their attractions could not withstand the adverse criticisms of their performances by the hotel speculators and agencies — that the fear of hot weather and war conditions might mean personal loss in case their eighteen front rows were not in the hands of the speculators through advance buy-outs.

If these managers could see the continuous line at the New Amsterdam box office and read the thousands of letters that I have received from my patrons they would know that the public has realized that the time has come when all managers must prevent their tickets from getting into the hands of the profiteers and the increase in their patronage will more than compensate them for the loss of their rake-off in dealing with speculators instead of direct with the theatre-going public. The managers are and have been too closely allied with the ticket profiteers for their own good.

THE TWENTIETH CENTURY THEATRE

The managers, I consider, are greatly to blame for driving the public away from the box office. The cry too long has been "the best we have is the eighteenth row," no matter for what week or day, or how far ahead, the purchaser wanted his ticket. They concluded, "Why go to the box office when you can't get what you want?"

Democracy is the leading theme of the day. We are giving our all to fight for it beyond the big pond. Why not establish it honestly in our home institutions? The theatre has done its bit in every other direction; why not make every person equal who applies for seats? Against the greatest odds I am glad to say I have successfully done so, as far as tickets for the *Ziegfeld Follies* and the *Ziegfeld Midnight Frolic* are concerned. Only this week I have turned down a buyout of 475 seats a night at a profit to me over box office prices of over $1700 weekly. The buyout assured me against any loss during the hot weather. I admit I am not in the theatrical business for my health, but I honestly believe that ticket profiteering if continued, means death to the theatre. . . .

The management of our big hotels of our great city, who I admit derive great benefit from the ticket agencies placed in their lobbies, could greatly help the present state of affairs by compelling these agencies to sell their tickets at a premium of not more than 50 cents over the box office price, but whether this ordinance is passed or not, tickets for *Ziegfeld Follies* are on sale and will be until the finish of the *Follies* run in New York, the 18th of September, and every seat from the first to the last row is on sale to those who come to the box office for them.

The theatres are compelled by the United States to stamp on each ticket the price at which that ticket is sold, and what I can't understand, or perhaps it has been overlooked by Uncle Sam, is why that same law does not apply to the ticket profiteer. Why is he allowed to take the very same ticket on which the price is stamped and sell it for more than the price stamped on its face? This is a phase of the controversy which has not been brought up. Believe me, I am in this fight to the finish, and if Alderman Quinn's ordinance is not passed, I am going to ascertain why the ticket-profiteer has privileges that are denied others. In a communication from District Attorney Swann, I am glad to learn he considered ticket speculating a non-essential industry, and the full resources of his office will be used under the anti-loafing law to stamp out every phase of it that his authority empowers him. Last Saturday night Assistant District Attorney Smith was in evidence on Forty-second Street and the "Diggers" were apprehended. The ticket speculators openly boast that I cannot last throughout the summer without them, but I believe the time has come when the public is awake on this subject and will not further tolerate it, and will refuse to attend those theatres which allow their tickets to fall into the hands of the agencies. A combination of manager and ticket speculator against the public is not tolerated in any other city. Why not unite now to wipe it out forever in New York and protect the public and amusement-seeking strangers who come to this great city for their entertainment?

If the price of seats at the theatre had risen as so many other things have risen, it would be most unfortunate. One essential element in the production of good plays is a certain amount of intelligence in the audience. Now for some reason

THE TWENTIETH CENTURY THEATRE

Divine Providence has not given to the majority of intelligent people unlimited cash. The ordinary well-educated man or woman must sacrifice something else he wants for everything he buys. The result of high prices in the theatre is simply to lower the intelligence of the audience, which in turn reacts on the proportion of cerebration revealed in the play and in the acting thereof. And, to compete with the moving pictures — which have helped in keeping down the price of theatre-seats — managers must make, except in musical comedy, some appeal to human intelligence. Suppose a man, his wife, and two daughters decide to witness a play; eight dollars gone at the start; and what Stevenson called the "leakage of travel" will probably raise it to ten. Indeed the man who can get himself and his family from the house or hotel to the theatre and back again, with no more expenditure than I have indicated, deserves to be called a financier. Now for ten dollars it is at least an even chance that the family will see a vulgar play, acted in a clumsy and perhaps silly fashion. And for those same ten dollars, the head of the house can purchase not merely one book, but a whole set of standard books, which will remain in the library permanently, and give instruction and delight to the third and fourth generations. Between these two alternatives, how long will a wise man hesitate? And I repeat that the eternal menace of the movies makes the theatre-manager reckon on a comparatively intelligent audience. This seems to me to supply one reason why the evil tendency of rising prices in the theatres failed to develop.

But the worst tendency in the early years of the twentieth century was the craze for the dramatisation of popular novels. This craze was finally killed by the blessed American sense of humour, but it wrought havoc in dramatic art during the days wherein it afflicted us. This particular fad had nothing whatever to do with the dramatisation of great works of fiction, which was common enough during the whole nineteenth century, and which will continue so long as the stage lasts. One of the most memorable performances of the 1917–1918 season was the production by the admirable French company of *Les Frères Karamazov*, a version of Dostoevski's masterpiece. Years ago, Mr. Sothern put on a play founded on another of Dostoevski's novels, *Crime and Punishment*. Mrs. Fiske made her first great success as an intellectual actress when she staged *Tess of the D'Urbervilles*. I was present on the second night, and there were only a handful of persons in the audience. But the dramatic critics told everybody not to miss it, and after the first week the house was packed.

THE TWENTIETH CENTURY THEATRE

Later she gave an interesting transcript from *Vanity Fair*. Such performances as these have no connexion with "best sellers," for they stand or fall entirely on their merits as acting plays.

The rage for the immediate transfer of the popular novel to the boards had a definite beginning. It began in 1894, with *Trilby* and *The Prisoner of Zenda*, and spread like a contagious disease. In a very short time, every "best seller" stalked before the footlights. Forty or fifty novels, already now quite forgotten, brought fortunes to the box-office. It made not the slightest difference whether or not the story had material adaptable to the stage. The only question was, Is everybody talking about it? Hall Caine used to sell the dramatic rights to his novels in advance of their publication, and nearly all writers of romances had their eyes on this enormous additional source of revenue as they composed their books. The climax was apparently reached when *Beside the Bonnie Briar Bush* was dramatised. Nearly every manager in New York employed a man whose sole tools of art were the scissors and the paste-pot. In an interesting interview in the New York *Sun* for October 14, 1900, an enterprising theatrical director remarked, "Six New York theatres are presenting plays made from books, and some thirty more works of fiction are to be transferred to the stage during the coming winter. . . . Fiction writers now work with one eye on the stage, and books are being read by actors and managers in the hope of finding there material. . . . The vogue of the dramatised novel seems likely to continue for some time to come, and it will be limited only by the number of popular novels that the authors turn out: I was about to say, so long as they continued to write novels that could be dramatised, but apparently no such distinction as that exists any longer. . . . I sometimes think that a capable man could dramatise the city directory well enough to make it a successful medium for a popular star." As has been said, this fad was killed by the American sense of humour, which is as potent in our country as bad art. A cartoon represented Dr. Johnson lamenting to Boswell his misfortune that he had not lived in a later time, for then his Dictionary would have been dramatised! Jennie Betts Hardwick, in a number of *Life*, wrote a *Ballad of the Modern Play*, of which the first stanza ran:

> When folk in this enlightened age
> >   Fare gaily forth to view the play,
> They see, adapted for the stage,
> >   The book they finished yesterday.
> Beneath the dramatiser's sway
> >   Its characters to being spring,
> They speak and move in lifelike way —
> >   The acted novel is the thing.

THE TWENTIETH CENTURY THEATRE

In January, 1901, I saw it seriously stated in a reputable journal that some managers kept a man on the railway trains to observe what novels had the largest sale.

But there is no doubt that the advance of the drama in America was checked by the dramatised novel. In an article in *The Independent* for April 8, 1897, I pointed out the peril. "Unless some lucky chance happens, the relation between these two forces of art may become as close and intimate in 1900 as it was in 1600. This will be very unfortunate for both. In the age of Elizabeth most dramatists did not invent their plots; they found ready material in histories, poems, and especially in contemporary romances. Shakespeare took the plot of *As You Like It* from Lodge's story *Rosalynde*, as he took the plot of *Winter's Tale* from Greene's *Pandosto*. But his motive was simple and blameless; he selected this material, not because it was popular, but because it was convenient. . . . But now we are in danger of losing what little original force our drama possesses, owing to the enormous financial returns realised from successfully dramatising a successful novel."

My fears were confirmed. Marie Corelli's story, *The Master Christian*, was acted as a play in America before the novel was published, so that there might be no quarrel as to the ownership of

THE TWENTIETH CENTURY THEATRE

the dramatic rights when the occasion came for the theatrical run. The vogue of the dramatised novel was founded on the desire of spectators to see favourite characters in popular books incarnate on the stage. When I attended the performance of *Trilby*, I remember the tremendous applause that greeted the three friends as they appeared arm in arm and before any one of them had uttered a word. This same desire was capitalised by shrewd managers in an analogous species of theatrical entertainment that flourished synchronously with the dramatised novel, and that was intrinsically no worse. This was the custom of making overnight actors out of prize-fighters like John L. Sullivan, James J. Corbett, Robert Fitzsimmons, James J. Jeffries, Kid McCoy, and many others — all of whom, with the exception of Mr. Corbett, who has some natural histrionic gift — were quite innocent of artistic ability. But these men were "in the public eye" and crowds paid money to see and hear these famous characters on the boards. From one point of view, it was worth the money. It is impossible to forget the shamefaced way in which the great John L. Sullivan said, "Mother, I'll take care of you now." Nor would I have missed for a good deal seeing Robert Fitzsimmons in *The Honest Blacksmith*. When the virtuous maiden was pursued by the designing villain,

Robert knocked him down, and the girl, throwing her arms around her saviour's neck, cried, "Oh Bob, God will reward you!" "Don't mention it," said Bob.

The point I make is that the mobilisation of prize-fighters as actors was not one whit worse than the transformation of popular books into plays. The same motive governed both.

It is interesting also to remember that the rage for the dramatised "best seller" degraded the American stage in another way; I mean by giving a new currency to that most artificial form, historical-costume-romantic-melodrama. After the success of *The Prisoner of Zenda*, the pseudo-romantic revival in English prose fiction flourished for ten years, from 1894 to 1904; during the same period came the vogue of the dramatised book, and quite naturally the easiest books to turn into plays were romances stuffed with incident, like *When Knighthood Was in Flower*, *Under the Red Robe*, *Janice Meredith*. For the first few years of our century romantic melodrama had its innings, as may be seen by a glance at the table printed in the first chapter. To-day nothing seems more obsolete than this. When, in the year 1915, Lou Tellegen produced *A King of Nowhere*, it seemed incredible that the audience were expected to take it seriously. To-day, with a few exceptions, melodrama will not succeed on the metropolitan stage unless it is mingled with humour, as in *Within the Law*, or unless it is frankly a farcical burlesque; there is a genuine field for melodramatic farce, though it must be done better than Granville Barker's contemptuous arrangement of Stevenson's *Wrong Box*. He was apparently trying to "get back" at the public for its lack of support of his most ambitious and — to my mind — magnificent productions; but his rebuke was less successful than his serious work. The present indifference to melodrama is perhaps the reason why Eugene Walter's play, *The Heritage*, failed in New York during the past season; it had much to commend it, there were some scenes of tremendous force, and it was remarkably well acted. It was apparently too horrible for the public, and too theatrical for the critics. I frankly confess that I enjoyed it, though it was on a lower level than the author's masterpiece, *The Easiest Way*.

From the death of these evil tendencies, which deserve recording in any sketch of twentieth century drama, it ought to be clear that the hope of the American stage is in original comedy, written on American themes by American authors. Such plays as *The Unchastened Woman* and *Why Marry*, and *The Copperhead* — the last-named glorified by the superb acting of Lionel Barrymore — point toward the true road. If we can keep to such standards, the time may come when our exports will actually exceed our imports. Between two visits that William Archer made to America in the twentieth century our drama sensibly advanced; he said that at his first visit nearly every successful play in New York was either an importation or an adaptation; at the second visit the best were original. We have already exported some plays to England — not always the best — and many to Australia. In the year 1916, of twenty-five produced in Melbourne, five were Australian, six English, one French, and thirteen American. Among the revivals were six other American plays. From the first of January to the first of April, 1917, in that city six new dramas were produced, every one of which came from America. Yet it should also be said, that according to the Melbourne correspondent of the Boston *Monitor*, "the only American play staged in eight years which left a memory of real artistic excellence is Clyde Fitch's *The Truth*."

In a letter written from London, October 5, 1916, published in the New York *Nation*, William Archer declared, "a large part of the British Drama is American, and what is not American is mainly idiotic. Looking down the column of theatrical advertisements, I find that the following American plays are running, all of them, I believe, with some measure of success: *Daddy Longlegs, Romance, Her Husband's Wife, The Misleading Lady, Mr. Manhattan, Broadway Jones, Potash and Perlmutter in Society* — and *Peg o' My Heart* has only just exhausted its enormous vogue."

Material and temporal things like cash and food often have a profound influence on things that are unseen and eternal. I am convinced that American and British drama would immediately gain in seriousness and become closer to the national life if Anglo-Saxons were willing to sacrifice the evening meal on the altar of art. In some parts of Europe the opera and the theatre are not intended mainly for the leisure class; they are regarded, not as a luxury, but as a necessity. It is assumed that the audience will be composed of persons who will have to get up at the usual hour the following morning, and do the day's work. In these localities long plays begin at seven, ordinary plays of ordinary length at half-past seven, and operas at six. There is a long pause after one of the acts, where those who have been unable to get anything to eat before the play, may obtain refreshment, while others who so wish may have a hearty supper after the performance, and still be in bed by eleven o'clock, a reasonable hour for beginning the night's rest. Furthermore the audience does not come to the theatre stupefied and soggy with the load of a heavy dinner. Their minds are alert, far better prepared to appreciate the best that art can offer.

I had hoped that war conditions in America would force our theatres to begin at seven, and close at ten or not much later; but alas! this happy arrangement only lasted in a few places for a short period, and then we went back to our old vices. Many Americans who travel to New York to see a play regard the whole expedition as a mild debauch; every visit to the theatre means a bad morning after. In England one of the chief foes of the drama is the English dinner, solemn, solid, and late; a heavy and brain-killing ordeal. Managers in London have been forced to begin later and later, and often to put on a curtain-raiser, during the performance of which the audience noisily find their places. The time of beginning caused so much serious reflection that on one occasion the London managers held a meeting, and then sent out a circular letter to a great many people, to enquire whether the dinner could be placed earlier, or the theatre still later in the night. The letter wound up with this question — At what hour should the curtain rise? A large variety of answers came in, some insisting on six, some on seven, and some on nine o'clock: a characteristic response was sent by Bernard Shaw — "For the majority of modern plays, the curtain should not rise at all."

The Anglo-Saxon custom of a "theatre-party," to which a considerable number of guests are invited, most of whom come late, finally sit down to a long and expensive banquet, eventually arriving at the theatre half an hour after the performance has begun, is about as helpful a preparation toward appreciating a good play as it would be toward competing in a mile run. I tremble to think what would happen to a man who should urge that opera in New York begin at six o'clock; yet the first performance of *Parsifal* in New York began at five, and Wagner operas at Covent Garden opened at the same hour. Plays that begin at half-past eight or nine with long intervals after each act, during which systematic arrangements are provided to erase the performance, can hardly make a deep impression. One reason why J. M. Barrie wrote *The Twelve Pound Look* in one act, was because he was determined not to be interrupted at a vital moment in the story.

III

THE DRAMA LEAGUE AND THE INDEPENDENT THEATRE

Effect of the Great War on the drama — three English witnesses — the Drama League — a contrast between two dramatists — George M. Cohan — the independent theatre — Little Theatres in the United States — Miss Mackay's book — Antoine — the Northampton municipal theatre — the Chicago little theatre — Washington Square players — Stuart Walker — Theodore Dreiser — Hull House, Chicago — Roland Holt — the laboratory theatre at Pittsburg — Franklin Sargent — the study of the theatre at American universities — George P. Baker — the Yale Dramatic Association — graduates of Harvard and Yale.

THE Great War, which has in so many places transformed triviality into seriousness, which has revealed everywhere so much sublime heroism in the minds of men and women, has certainly not elevated the theatre. It seems particularly unfortunate that just at the time when we have so many able dramatists in both England and America, the level of excellence on the London and New York stage should be so low. The war is not to blame for this; the people are to blame. In order to understand why it is that during days wherein we are all witnessing the greatest drama in human history, the theatres for the most part furnish silliness and vulgarity, we must remember that before the war the mass of Englishmen and Americans looked upon play-going merely as a form of entertainment. Only the other day a man said to a minister of the Gospel, "Since this war began in 1914 I have ceased to believe in God." The minister replied, "Did you believe in Him before the war?"

If dramatic art before 1914 had been a recognised part of national life and of the education of the people, had it even played so important a part as orchestral music and grand opera, we should never have allowed it to sink during the war. In the year 406 B.C., toward the end of the long struggle between Athens and Sparta, when it was plain that Athens was hopelessly beaten, and the bitter end was near, Euripides put on the Athenian stage one of his greatest masterpieces. Great art will live even amid national distress. But if the people regard the theatre as a place of light entertainment, where they check their brains with their overcoats before entering the auditorium, then in time of war they will naturally seek even lighter entertainment as a relief from the all-enveloping shadow. It has not yet occurred to them that the best relief from real tragedy is another form of elevation, another form of intense mental activity, rather than brain-shattering nonsense. Mr. Gladstone, Lord Morley, Mr. Balfour, and other English statesmen found the best change from absorbing political activities in mental work of another sort, rather than in something silly or base. In order to prove that I am not painting the picture in too dark colours, I should like to call to the witness stand three authoritative and patriotic testifiers.

In the New York *Nation* for November 9, 1916, William Archer wrote from London, "As for the English productions, a selection of titles, will, I think, justify my description of the majority of them [as idiotic]: *High Jinks, Pell Mell, This and That, A Little Bit of Fluff, Woman and Wine, Ye Gods! Some, The Bing Boys are Here, Look Who's Here, Razzle-Dazzle! The Girl from Ciro's.* Most of these productions are 'revues,' making no pretension to sanity; and the remainder are farces of brainless and degraded cynicism. Nor is the tale of triviality exhausted in this list; for several pieces which do not proclaim their idiocy in their titles are in fact as idiotic as the rest." He adds, "Gen. Smith-Dorrien made some sensation by denouncing the evil from the moral point of view. But there is, in truth, much more imbecility than vice in the matter. It is a curious fact — due, I think, to a long sequence of historical causes — that in England many people of more than average intelligence in every other respect become imbeciles the moment they approach the theatre."

THE TWENTIETH CENTURY THEATRE

In a number of the London *Times*, commenting on the 1916 season, the critic wrote, "it would almost seem as if the war had had a stultifying effect on the playwright's imagination," and followed up this statement with a pessimistic review of the year.

In the London *Athenæum* for August, 1917, under the caption *The Theatre We Deserve*, a thoughtful writer begins as follows: "Whatever the War has ennobled, its purifying flame has at least left the English theatre unscorched. Triviality remains its characteristic note, with overtones of the lighter pornography. . . . But we need not flatter ourselves that it is war which has made our theatre trivial; it has at the most emphasised an already established tradition . . . the fault lies not with the actor-managers and business managers, or the mistresses of theatrical speculators, or the playwrights, or even with the high ground-rents and subcontracting manipulations, but primarily with the audiences. These other factors have an influence, serious and often degrading, but indirect. The main trouble is the body of playgoers — a conclusion which is, of course, a platitude analogous to that which declares that a nation has the government, the press, the priests, it deserves."

The *Athenæum* writer has a remedy, which it is

pleasant to remember, is already in America an accomplished fact, and which is bound to help the stage. "To the writer it seems perfectly possible as a step to a better theatre to organise an audience . . . a wide, loosely knitted theatre society could be formed which would rally round such managers as should be courageous enough to attempt the play which is approved by their artistic conscience, but now commonly declined because it is not what (they assume) the public wants . . . Such a theatre society is in process of being formed, and the *Athenæum* would be glad to put any inquirers in touch with the venturesome optimists who are putting themselves at the heroic pains to organise it."

This society, known as the Drama League, has a healthy existence in the United States. In the comparative absence of repertory theatres, with nearly every town lacking a stock company, its efforts have not been as fruitful as they might be with a better system of play-production. But the League is gradually spreading sound doctrine, and its main work is devoted to the education of audiences. Both managers and dramatists are glad to have the League's endorsement; it means increased business. The League flourishes in every part of America. I have attended enthusiastic and crowded meetings in Chicago, New Orleans,

Birmingham, Pittsburgh, and many other cities. The League is a vital force, and its influence is steadily widening and deepening.

The members of the League are not easily discouraged. This is fortunate, for the difficulties in the way of progress are enormous. Besides the general inertia in the road of any reform, they must count on the hostility of many managers, some of whom not only wish no reform, but sincerely believe that dramatic criticism should be abolished; and they must count on the cynical attitude of the popular playwright who makes his income by catering to the public taste. He will point to his own success with complacent superiority, and regard every attempt to elevate the drama as the work of penniless cranks ignorant of true theatrical conditions. Nay, he will insist that all those who wish better plays on the stage mean by that goal nothing but boredom. Verily I say unto you, he has his reward. He means to keep it too.

For an excellent illustration of what I mean by a popular playwright who is only a caterer, I select a pleasant gentleman who speaks with frankness and modesty of his own work. So far as I know he has never written anything vulgar or debasing, and I am quite sure that the main object of his life — which is to please theatre audiences — would never lead him into any line of work that he thought degrading. He is respectable, and not because it pays, either, but because socially he is a respectable man. But the trouble with him is that he is first, last, and all the time an entertainer. He has pleased many grown-up children so long that it has apparently never dawned upon him that there is something in the theatre more interesting than lively talk and amusing situations. I refer of course to Ideas, which his plays not only do not possess, but which, in any connexion with the theatre, he has not even considered.

On a visit, at the height of his success, to New York, he granted an interview to the *Times*. He was of course, only half-serious, like his plays. Here are some of the things he said with a pleasant smile. When the newspaper representative asked him about the failure of good plays and the success of trash, he remarked, "I don't know what on earth it means. It seems to me to have extremely little sense in it. Once in a hundred times, when a play is a failure, it fails because it is over the heads of the audience. The ninety-nine other times it fails because it is beneath the audience's contempt . . . It is most unfair to abuse the managers and dramatists for any such state of affairs. You must abuse your public. The public gets what it asks for . . . Personally, I don't want to be uplifted, but I dare say there are people who do.

THE TWENTIETH CENTURY THEATRE

The only thing I resent is that they should ask me to uplift them. . . . To write a play requires no intellectual ability. It is well to have intellectual ability, but not essential. You can write a play if you have the knack of getting what you have to say over the footlights. And Heaven only knows what that knack is and how it comes. Fortunately, only a very few have it, and those who have are able to keep the wolf from the door — and live in the St. Regis," said he, with a twinkle.

The next year, on the Continent, I had a talk with one of the greatest dramatists of our time, a man who has profoundly influenced not only the stage, but also modern thought. And yet the majority of his plays have been failures on the stage, because he has in each case tried for something original, something that had not before been attempted. I asked him whether his numerous failures distressed him very much, and he replied, "The true artist, the true dramatist, must not think of the box-office while he is writing his plays. He must express himself, which is the only reason for writing at all. If what he writes happens to be financially successful, so much the better. But he must not think of popular success while he is at work."

The difference between these two men is the difference between failure in success and success in failure. The first man is a facile playwright, who makes a fortune by following the public taste. He never has been a leader, he never will be, and apparently is contented not to be. The stage is his livelihood, a pleasant and respectable way of earning a living. But his influence on the stage, and on modern drama, and on modern thought, is precisely zero. The second man has missed the target more times than he has hit it, because his target is a difficult one. But his few hits have made him one of the greatest figures in the world of literature and thought, and his misses have been more instructive than most hits. He commands the intellectual respect of the world, and it would be impossible to write the history of European drama without emphasising his efforts.

But it is a mistake to suppose that a successful play must necessarily be devoid of cerebration. Sir Arthur Pinero, who has often descended to what he apparently at the moment thought was the popular level, has earned his justly high reputation as a dramatist when he has given the best of his thought as well as of his technique to the undertaking. *The Second Mrs. Tanqueray*, *His House in Order*, and *The Thunderbolt* are more often associated with his name than *The Wife without a Smile*. In the field of the novel, Arnold Bennett's position depends upon *The Old Wives' Tale* rather than on his numerous pot-boilers. There are many dramatists and novelists who think it unfair when they are abused by the critics for producing trash. They say, "But, my dear sir, I don't profess to uplift the public. All I am trying to do is to make a living. And I am making a remarkably good one. Why is it not just as respectable to earn money by making plays to fill a popular demand, as it is to make shoes?" But the critics — and the critics are simply the conscience of the public — will never forgive a man for doing less than his best. The maker of shoes, if he succeeds, is presumably doing his best; the maker of theatrical entertainment, when he succeeds, may be revealed only as a traitor to his higher self.

I remember George M. Cohan, in one of his old-time flag-dances, with every seat in the house taken, singing a topical song ridiculing the critics. He pointed to himself with a contagious laugh, saying

> The rich are growing richer

and then, pointing to the struggling musicians in the orchestra —

> The poor are growing poorer.

But Mr. Cohan went forward when he decided to change from dancing to play-writing. And it

THE TWENTIETH CENTURY THEATRE

may be that he will some day decide to reach that place to which his talents must constantly invite him. It may seem absurd for me to suggest that so successful, so apparently cheerful a person as Mr. Cohan is at heart discontented. Nevertheless, I am sure, that with his genuine ability, there are times when he is dissatisfied. Not dissatisfied with his income; I mean dissatisfied with himself. No man with brains ever lives long in the temperature of complacency.

Evidences for better days in the American theatre are not always to be found in the long runs of popular plays. They are to be found in more obscure but more veritable signs of promise. The increase in the number of stock companies, the growth of municipal theatres, the development of the Little Theatres, the influence of the Drama League, the widespread and remarkable interest taken in university courses on modern drama — all of these stimulate hope.

Constance Mackay, in her admirable book, *The Little Theatre in the United States*, says, "Northampton, Mass., has the only Municipal Theatre in the United States." But the tiny town of Lewes in Delaware has supported for some years a successful municipal theatre. It was erected by public subscription, is managed by a commission, and affords the citizens opportunities to hear good plays

THE TWENTIETH CENTURY THEATRE

performed by resident talent and by visiting companies. There is a municipal theatre in Colorado, and there are probably others. In Canada, Port Arthur has had one for a long time. But the first and most important one in America is at Northampton, and the experiment has helped to make the town famous. It was an ideal place to make the trial, for there are nearly two thousand girls in Smith College. It started in 1892 through the generosity of Mr. E. H. R. Lyman, and twenty years later was reorganised. The theatre is owned and the support of the company guaranteed by the city. Each week a new play is given, and the best travelling companies are invited thither. Being called before the curtain after a performance of *Hamlet*, Mr. Forbes-Robertson said, "No matter what it costs you, do not give up your Municipal Theatre."

Miss Mackay's book should be consulted by all who are interested in the growth of little theatres and repertory theatres in America. It was published in 1917, and the first sentence of the preface has a triumphant ring. "This book aims to give a complete survey of one of the newest, freest, most potent, and democratic forces in the art of the American stage — the Little Theatre."

The idea of the Little Theatre came from one of the ablest and shrewdest managers in the world,

THE TWENTIETH CENTURY THEATRE

Antoine of Paris, who has succeeded in all his undertakings except when he tried, at the request of the State, to direct that famous old barn by the Luxembourg, the Odéon, hallowed in the memories of thousands of students in the Quarter. Paris theatres are exceedingly dirty, possibly because they are open seven nights in the week, and the Odéon was the dirtiest of all. He spent months cleaning and restoring it, he sat down in every bad seat in the structure to see if a good view of the stage were obtainable; if it were not, he had the seat removed. Possibly a man of his independence could not accommodate himself to State control; I suspect he was often homesick for his own theatre on the Boulevard, the Théâtre Antoine, where the best seats used to sell for five francs, and where he himself acted in *King Lear*, *Ghosts*, and many contemporary pieces.

It was in 1887 that he made his epoch-making experiment. Miss Mackay quotes the late Jules Lemaître: "We had the air of good Magi in mackintoshes seeking out some lowly but glorious manger. Can it be that in this manger the decrepit and doting drama is destined to be born again!" She adds, "Lemaître's words were prophetic. Had he been, in his feuilleton, even more prophetic, he might have pointed out that André Antoine by establishing the first genuine Little Theatre the world had ever seen was to influence the art of the stage more profoundly than any man of his generation."

I will myself pay another tribute to Antoine by saying that it was largely owing to his efforts that the great name of Henry Becque was rescued from forgetfulness, and his masterpieces restored to the stage.

From the initial Free Theatre of Antoine in 1887 sprang the Little Theatre idea that spread gradually over Europe, and reached the United States in the season of 1911–1912. According to Miss Mackay, "Out of fifty-five Little Theatres in the United States there have been four failures." An impressive record.

Not only have our American Little Theatres raised the standard of acting and stage presentation, but they have made a home for one-act plays, analogous to the art of the short-story in prose fiction. The attempt of the Princess Theatre in New York to imitate the Grand Guignol in Paris by combining short horrors with short farces faded away, partly because the American public was not sufficiently seasoned, partly because the attempt lacked dramatic sincerity. But other undertakings, even though some of them have become temporarily bankrupt, had notable results. Chief among these is Maurice Browne's Chicago Little Theatre, The

Washington Square and The Greenwich Village players in New York, and the whole work of Stuart Walker, first as originator and director of the Portmanteau Theatre, and then as Director of orthodox successful plays.

The Chicago theatre produced plays by Euripides, Ibsen, Strindberg, Shaw, Houghton, Hankin, Dunsany, Yeats — a long list of bold experiments. It is not too much to say that Maurice Browne quickened the intellectual life of Chicago. The Washington Square players, starting as amateurs, graduated into professionals, leased a regular theatre, and gave performances both exotic and indigenous, that attracted the attention of the whole country. As I am writing this paragraph, they are playing in San Francisco. Of their original American pieces, nothing impressed me more than Susan Glaspell's one-act *Trifles*, an absolutely truthful tragedy of farm life, exceedingly well acted. This play gives Miss Glaspell a high place among American dramatists.

Stuart Walker is a remarkable combination of idealism and common sense. No director has higher aims than he, or shows better judgment in their attainment. He founded his now famous Portmanteau Theatre — where the scenery is carried about with the company and can be set up in a few moments either out or indoors — in the season of 1915-1916. One of his most notable performances is *Gammer Gurton's Needle*, a splendid, rollicking, English university farce of the sixteenth century. In the winter of 1917-1918 he produced in New York *The Book of Job* in a beautiful and dignified manner. Fortunately at the same time he mounted one of the most successful plays in America, a dramatisation of Booth Tarkington's *Seventeen*. Nothing pleased me more than the run of this delightful comedy, for I knew that it meant something more than money to Mr. Walker. It meant freedom — a free hand to go ahead with things closer to his heart. He told me so between the acts. I rejoice in his youth; he ought to have a long career and to accomplish great things for American drama.

Mr. Jewett, with his company of repertory players at the small Copley Theatre in Boston, has produced many excellent dramas in an excellent way; and the interesting experiments made by the Little Theatre of Indianapolis, which was founded in 1915, have excited lovers of theatrical art throughout the whole country. Mr. Samuel A. Eliot, Jr., was the first director, and set a high standard which his successors have attempted to maintain. Here was given the first performance on any stage of a play by an Indiana man — Theodore Dreiser — a play, too, that seemed in theory impossible. Mr. Dreiser's volume of original pieces, *Plays of the Natural and Supernatural*, seems to me so superior in every way to the majority of his novels, that I wish he were only a playwright. This particular experiment was *Laughing Gas*, put on in 1916. According to Mr. Oliver M. Sayler, who wrote a long account of the performance in the Boston *Transcript* for December 22, 1916, "the achievement in the effective production of *Laughing Gas* amounts to the vivid presentation simultaneously on the same stage in alternate episodes and rhythms of both the natural and the supernatural." Mr. Dreiser deserves credit for having written one of the most original plays of the twentieth century; and the Little Theatre of Indianapolis deserves credit for successfully surmounting apparently insurmountable obstacles in the performance. I would give much to have seen it.

One of the hopeful signs of the times is the Settlement Theatre, of which the most significant is at Hull House, Chicago. The players were organised as far back as 1900, and the interest has never waned. They have produced plays covering dramatic history from Ben Jonson to Barrie. Possibly their highest point was reached with Galsworthy's *Justice*, given in 1911, long before Americans had any opportunity to see it on the professional stage.

THE TWENTIETH CENTURY THEATRE

A gentleman who has studied the modern drama for years wrote me on the night of April 26, 1911, "I have just come back from Hull House . . . where I went to see a performance of Galsworthy's *Justice*. It was one of the most astounding presentations I have ever seen. . . . The acting of the parts — by the members of the various Hull House Clubs — was wonderful."

The publisher, Mr. Roland Holt, who has been actively identified with the Drama League, and who has made a special study of the independent theatre in America, says that there are now (June, 1918) sixty Little Theatres in the United States. I will quote the rest of his recently delivered speech, word for word, because it proves two things: first that there are to-day many opportunities to hear good plays, if one will look for them; second, that if a large body of theatre-goers should follow Mr. Holt's example, the business of the regular Broadway entertainment might be considerably notched.

In my own case, I have spent twenty-one evenings in the thirty-eight weeks since the middle of August at independent theatres, against twenty-five at Broadway shows. Six of these evenings were at the Washington Square Players, who, to my thinking at least, are the most hopeful and important movement on our American stage. I have to thank them for plays by Shaw and Benevente, by O'Neill and Glaspell. I gave four evenings to Miss Grace Griswold's Theatre Workshop, the most ideal plan of them all,

THE TWENTIETH CENTURY THEATRE

and enjoyed plays by Synge and Björnson; three evenings at the Neighborhood Theatre in Grand Street gave me the Wisconsin Players in their own plays, and other actors in Browning and Dunsany; four evenings at Mr. Conroy's Greenwich Village Theatre included Schnitzler, Hewlett, and one of O'Neill's masterly sea plays. My other independent evenings included one at the Vieux Colombier, one at the Provincetown Players, a Sunday night benefit performance of three war plays, one at Northampton's delightful Municipal Theatre, and one with plays by Schnitzler and Marjorie Patterson (whose Pierrot the Prodigal we've all enjoyed) at the tiny Vagabond Playhouse in Baltimore, which seats less than seventy.

I was pleased by a visit to the Laboratory Theatre of the Carnegie Institute at Pittsburg in April, 1917. This is a beautiful auditorium, with adjoining workshops where everything concerned with the art of acting and the art of stage-presentation may be effectively studied. The Institute gives the degree of Bachelor of Arts in the Drama, and the productions include specimens from the whole range of dramatic literature, ancient and contemporary. Graduates of this school may raise the standard of professional acting in America.

Before speaking of the contribution to the advance of the drama made by our universities, it is well to pay homage to an American who I think has never received anything like sufficient credit for his services. This is Franklin Sargent, head of the American Academy of Dramatic Arts, in New York. The college revivals of Elizabethan plays, which have become a feature of extra-curriculum activities in every quarter of the United States, had their origin and impulse in a performance of Ben Jonson's *Silent Woman*, given in the winter of 1894–1895 by the pupils of Mr. Sargent, and under his direction. Since that epoch-making night, he has not only revived many old plays, but given New Yorkers their only opportunity to see some famous modern ones, like Tolstoi's *Power of Darkness* and Becque's *Les Corbeaux*. Furthermore he frequently stages pieces by American authors.

Among the large number of American university professors who have stimulated interest in the theatre, one man will be universally recognised as deserving first mention — Professor George Pierce Baker, of Harvard. His famous course in playwriting, to which it is a signal honour to be admitted as a student, is eminently practical; and the laboratory performances of the plays give opportunities for the art of acting, the art of presentation, and the art of criticism. I can only wonder at the ability of Professor Baker to endure the prodigious labour involved by the direction of the Harvard Workshop, but he ought to be satisfied by the splendid results achieved. His pupils carry back with them to their homes in every part of America a fine enthusiasm for the theatre, which appears in many different directions. Some of the prize plays have been seen on the metropolitan stage; and among his former students are successful playwrights like Edward Sheldon, Edward Knoblauch, Jules Goodman, and Josephine Peabody. In 1918 two volumes of *Harvard Plays* were published, with valuable editorial comment by the Master of the Show.

One of the immediate outgrowths of the Harvard Idea was the laboratory theatre at Dartmouth, where, in the summer, under the direction of Mr. Jack Crawford of Yale, a number of interesting plays are given.

Courses on contemporary drama are now a regular part of the curriculum in most American universities; and to supply the students with material, many collections of modern plays have been published. The object of these courses is not to train playwrights, *but to train audiences*. It is to give to the young men an unquenchable thirst for good drama, so that they will be satisfied only with the best. Nearly every college graduate is a theatre-goer; hence the development of good taste and critical ability is a legitimate and important part of a college education.

In addition to the work done in college courses,

there is, in many universities, a student Dramatic Association, whose extra-curriculum activity is confined to the presentation and acting of high-class drama. One of the first and most important of these is the Yale University Dramatic Association, founded by Harry D. Wescott in 1899; its constitution has been copied in many other places. The object of the Yale players is to produce only dramas that, first, belong to literature, and second, cannot as a rule be seen on the professional stage. (The so-called Dramatic Societies in our universities that produce musical burlesques and farces written by students have no place in this book, and it is my opinion they should have no place in any institution of learning, as their efforts represent a sheer waste of time.) Among the plays produced by the Yale Association for the first time in American history, are Thomas Heywood's *Fair Maid of the West;* Shakespeare's *Troilus and Cressida;* Gogol's *Revizor* (first time anywhere in English); Ibsen's *Pretenders* (first time anywhere in English); curiously enough, William Archer, who wrote the translation, had never had any opportunity to hear it on the stage until the Yale performance, when he happened to be in America. Among other plays infrequently produced, the Yale Association gave Shakespeare's *King Henry IV, Part I*, Oliver Goldsmith's *The Good-Natured Man*, Goldoni's *The*

Fan, and the old *Second Shepherd's Play*. Student-members of the association who afterwards became identified with the professional stage are Charles Hopkins, the Director of the Punch and Judy Theatre in New York; Maxwell Parry, a member of the Washington Square Players; Thomas Achelis, who appeared in the New York presentation of Edward Sheldon's *Romance;* and Charles Templeton Crocker, who wrote one of the plays for the Bohemian Club in San Francisco.

IV

THE BIBLE AND POETRY ON THE STAGE

Recrudescence of the Mystery Play — the Bible on the modern stage — *Salomé* — *Joseph and his Brethren* — *The Book of Job* — Morality Plays — revival of *Everyman* — results of this — possibility of modern verse drama — Stephen Phillips — Continental poetic drama — the opportunity.

ONE interesting feature of twentieth century drama has been the notable increase in the use of the Bible as dramatic material. This is a curious recrudescence of the Mystery Play — a return to the origins of the modern theatre. Our modern drama began in mediæval times by the introduction into the liturgical church service of some episode taken from the Bible. Out of this developed the *Mysteries*, many survivals of which can be found to-day in Spain, Mexico, and other countries, whilst the most remarkable of all is of course the Passion Play of Oberammergau, given every tenth year. Whether the large number — and they are surprisingly numerous — of modern "passion plays" has had anything to do with the growing use of the Bible as quarry for the dramatist, I do not know; possibly just the contrary is a stronger factor, I mean the secularisation of the Sacred Books. Whatever the cause, the fact is that Mystery Plays have come to life again, and many modern playwrights simply take a story from the Bible, add or subtract as they please, and a new play is born.

One of the first of these, one of the most famous, and one that still holds the boards, is *Salomé*, by Oscar Wilde, 1893. This was written in French for Sarah Bernhardt. The censor forbade its production in London, but it has since appeared in many languages on the European and American stage; its renown was increased and accelerated in operatic form. The play is a powerful work of genius, and when competently staged and acted exceedingly impressive. It was shortly followed by Sudermann's *Johannes* (1898) at first forbidden in Berlin as sacrilegious! Straining at gnats and swallowing camels seems to be one of the characteristics of the Teutonic mind. Meanwhile in 1897 Rostand produced in Paris his beautiful *La Samaritaine: Evangile en trois tableaux*. This has had a number of Holy Week revivals, and was played by Mme. Bernhardt in New York. At about the same year in the twentieth century Maeterlinck the Belgian and Heyse the German each wrote a play on Mary Magdalene; Mrs. Fiske appeared in America in Heyse's drama, and Maeterlinck's was

THE TWENTIETH CENTURY THEATRE

produced at the New Theatre. In France, Antoine staged at the Odeón the story of Esther, perhaps the most dramatic of the books of the Old Testament; the French version unfortunately was merely a gorgeous, bloody melodrama. Ella Wheeler Wilcox has written a play on the same theme, but the really great tragedy imprisoned in the old text has not yet emerged. Stephen Phillips's successful *Herod* may properly be called a Bible play. Louis Parker made a highly interesting spectacle out of *Joseph and His Brethren*, which had a long run in New York; the American poet, Richard Burton, wrote a play *Rahab*, which was produced in Chicago; John Masefield has recently published *Good Friday;* while one of the most interesting dramatic performances in New York in 1918 was Stuart Walker's *The Book of Job*. In this striking performance, both the poetic language and the dramatic situations obtained their full value — so far as was possible on the stage — while the amount of legitimate humour in the old book was revealed to many for the first time. There is no doubt that we are to behold an increasing number of Biblical plays; one can find plenty of good material in the *Apocrypha*.

The immense success of Ben Greet's production of *Everyman*, with Miss Edith Wynne Mathison as Death, not only gave modern audiences some

THE TWENTIETH CENTURY THEATER

notion of what the effect of that Morality Play must have been on devout believers centuries ago, but led to the writing of a number of religious plays, somewhat akin to the old Moralities, of which the two most famous are *The Servant in the House* and *The Passing of the Third Floor Back*. Less successful were attempts to write straight modern Moralities, like *Everywoman* and *Experience*, the latter of which is sadly oversentimentalised. If Bernard Shaw's *Androcles and the Lion* is not religious, his Preface assuredly is.

As to the often-discussed question of the possibility of acting modern English plays in verse, nothing important can be said for or against in the abstract. If a genius appears who elects the verse-form, we shall all see another illustration of Kipling's phrase, "when the thing that couldn't has occurred." Our greatest English dramatic tradition is verse; and when the properly-trained company appears, we find nothing artificial or difficult in Shakespeare's poetry on the stage. In the nineteenth century, Tennyson wrote most of his plays in verse, and their failure was not due to their form. Browning's *Blot in the 'Scutcheon*, and *In a Balcony*, are decidedly convincing when well acted; they stand out bright in my memory. Miss Peabody's *The Piper* is one of the most successful plays in English of our century; and the verse-form gave the audience no trouble, because it troubled the actors not at all.

When Stephen Phillips's drama *Herod* was originally produced in London in 1900, many believed that the dawn of the poetry-play had begun. "It will take oysters and champagne to recover from this," a hardened theatre-goer remarked between the acts. One of our best American critics, John Corbin, writing from London to *Harper's Weekly*, started off by saying, "To imagine that one has seen the dawning of a new and brighter day in art or in literature is easy — dangerously easy; but in witnessing the performance of Mr. Stephen Phillips's *Herod* it is perhaps more difficult to persuade oneself that one has not. I do not use the words lightly. A new day in the poetical drama of England means something that has not been witnessed since the decay of the School of Shakespeare. There have been plays in verse and to spare from Dryden to Sheridan Knowles — or let us say to Comyns Carr; but I do not know of any of them that has revealed a genuine poet of the stage."

Later, in the year 1909, I witnessed in America a memorable performance of *Herod* by William Faversham and Julie Opp; the full beauty of the lines was rendered, and the whole production generously splendid. There were not a few dramatic moments. I should like to see it again. Yet we know now that Mr. Phillips was neither the morning-star nor the sunrise; it was another case of false dawn. And the reason? Simply because Stephen Phillips was more poet than dramatist.

It does seem strange when we consider first, that the glory of the English language is its poetry, that English writers have contributed to the literature of the world more high class poetry than that supplied from any other nation, that the greatest dramatist in all history was an English poet; and second, that the most famous play by a contemporary Frenchman and by a contemporary German is in each case in verse — *Cyrano de Bergerac* and *Die versunkene Glocke* — that we cannot have successful serious English plays in the poetic form.

It may be that the Great War will inspire some now unknown dramatist to write some colossal verse drama. Thomas Hardy, in *The Dynasts*, created a poetic drama of epic grandeur, and Granville Barker put some of it on the stage; but it can hardly be called a stage-play. Now out of this war, so much more universal in its reach than the Napoleonic struggle, some genius ought to find a subject made to his hand. I respectfully request those who attempt the task not to send me their productions in manuscript.

V

SHAKESPEARE ON THE MODERN STAGE

Shakespeare on the modern stage — the love of children for Shakespeare — his influence on uncultivated minds — the "Old Vic." — Japanese performance and criticism of *Othello* — realism in Shakespeare's dialogue — the tercentenary year in New York — Richard Mansfield — Salvini — the New Theatre production of *Winter's Tale* — Robert Mantell — Shakespeare on the art of acting — Hamlet — necessity of trained companies.

THE best comedies and tragedies of William Shakespeare will always hold the stage, because they are the most interesting and the most dramatic plays in the history of literature. Any child old enough to talk will enjoy them; and no octogenarian can outgrow them. All children should be brought up on Shakespeare; they should read him in the original, not in a novelised form. I had read every one of his plays before I was twelve years old. My taste at that time was not particularly discriminating, for I thought his masterpiece was *Titus Andronicus*. I liked that melodrama because, in the twentieth century vernacular, it had the "punch." I used to talk about Shakespeare with my aunt every morning; she rose at the voice of the bird, and we used to discuss Shakespeare from five until seven. I remember her saying that Shakespeare had a profound knowledge of the human heart. That remark made little impression on me, for at that time I knew and cared nothing about the human heart; all I knew was that Shakespeare was the greatest teller of stories that I had ever read, and that his characters were interesting folks. If older persons would discuss Shakespeare with children, they would help to educate the young, and they would receive much independent and original Shakespearean criticism. Furthermore, children should be taken to Shakespeare performances — on the few occasions when such things happen — at a tender age. I was not permitted to go to the theatre until I was eighteen; and although my first experience was an atrocious performance of *Macbeth* by Thomas W. Keene, who slid around the stage as though he were on roller skates, I enjoyed it unspeakably, and learned much. The first time I witnessed *Hamlet* the melancholy prince was interpreted by the worst actor in the world, the ex-Rev. George C. Miln, of Chicago. He copiously illustrated every fault mentioned in Hamlet's advice to the players, and yet even through that caricature many things in the play that had previously seemed to me confused became clear and stimulating.

I believe that even on uncultivated natures

THE TWENTIETH CENTURY THEATRE

Shakespeare makes a deeper impression than any other dramatist. A number of years ago Mr. Sothern and Mr. Mansfield simultaneously presented a Shakespearean play in New York; Sothern appeared in *Hamlet*, Mansfield in *Julius Cæsar*. I wrote an article about them in *The Independent*, and a short time after, I received the following letter, which I here transcribe *verbatim et literatim;* omitting only the name of the man and that of the town from which he wrote.

—, Alabama, 3-23-1903.

To Professor Lampson:

While at my leasure our to day I chance to read the Independent Weekly Magazine and I seen a sketch of a play that I seen about 12 years a go at the capital Theater in Little Rock ark and it is my desire to read it over What will the three acts cost me and can I purchas them from you are can you are rather will you let me no what house I can get it from and the cost of it excuse me the name of the play was Hamlets. At pres I works in the office of the L & N. co but have some knowledge of the play and if I get it I and several others will take a part and see what and amt we can make in little towns please let me no in Return mail and oblige

Tolstoi might have cancelled his book on Shakespeare had he seen this letter. For here is a man who knew nothing of Shakespeare's reputation, who had no idea what he ought to like or ought not to like, but who, after the lapse of twelve years, remembered with pleasure a performance of *Hamlet*. I hope he acted in it, and I would have paid any price for a ticket; this man and his company would have given us an interpretation quite untrammelled by tradition.

And how many times have I wished that I might see a Shakespeare play without knowing the plot! One September night in 1890, I sat in the gallery at Birmingham, England, and enjoyed Wilson Barrett's playing of *Hamlet* through the minds of my companions, who were all unskilled labourers. They had no idea how the play was "coming out" (how I envied them!) and they followed it with breathless attention. When Hamlet caught the King at prayer, one of them whispered "Now he's going to kill him!" and his disappointment at Hamlet's flimsy reasoning was plain to see. Once sitting in the top gallery at a performance of *Romeo and Juliet*, I had an opportunity to see what havoc Mercutio can make in a gentle bosom. The gallant gentleman was borne off dying, and in a moment Romeo rushed on seeking revenge. As the young hero attacked Tybalt, a girl near me ejaculated, "I hope he kills him!" She was shaking with excitement, for like all of us, she loved Mercutio. I wish that Walter De La Mare could have heard her.

The "Old Vic.," at Newington Butts, London —

famous spot in the history of the British stage — after all kinds of vicissitudes, gave many Shakespeare performances in the twentieth century under the management of Ben Greet; the wild enthusiasm of the uncultivated audience was a refreshing spectacle both to actors and critics.

Early in the twentieth century there was a Japanese performance of *Othello* in Tokio, given by a famous local company that had returned from a European tour. It is interesting to see how Shakespeare's tragedy, acted by Japanese players in the Japanese language, affected a native audience, who judged it apart from our literary standards. The regular dramatic critic published a long account of it in a Japanese paper, dated February 25, 1903, which has been translated for me by a Japanese friend.

OTHELLO AT THE MEIJI-ZA

It must be acknowledged that *Othello*, recently performed at the Meiji-Za has, to a certain extent, satisfied the thirst of the pleasure seekers of the whole city. . . . We fully appreciate the noble effort resulting in the selection of one of old Shakespeare's four great tragedies, the stage representation of which, evincing as it did the thoughtfulness and care on the part of those who took part in it, was received with satisfaction, though partial, by the spectators. . . .

In short, the Kawakami company has brought home from Europe such stage outfits as our eyes had never be-

THE TWENTIETH CENTURY THEATRE

held, in order to present to us, with the cream of the actors and the actresses of the new school, the great tragedy, *Othello*. Of Shakespeare's great tragedies, *Othello* is, indeed, the only one that can be easily made over into a play appreciable by our national habit of life. Even then, it includes a great deal of the Christian ideas and thoughts more or less strange to us, and the customs of those days were very different from to-day. It will be interesting, therefore, to follow Kawakami and his assistants in their efforts to overcome these difficulties.

. . . the occidental tone has been by no means wholly got rid of: . . . the marriage of Desdemona and Lieutenant-General Othello in the little chapel after she had run away from her father's house, all of which goes by the name love and its sacredness: "Have you prayed to-night?" being Othello's words spoken to Desdemona on the night of the murder: his most extravagant cries of anguish when he learned the innocence of his wife, whom Emilia called an angel — all these were bound to arouse the feeling of strangeness in the minds of our spectators.

Nay, more in the European play, as a rule, speeches play the most important rôle in contrast with gestures in ours. The success of the performance is measured by the degree of skill by which emotions are expressed by the speeches. The translated *Othello*, due to the original, of course, is rich in long speeches. One of the best illustrations of this is Iago's seducing speech to the Lieutenant-General in the garden. The subtlety of the art involved in this part is one of those points in the whole play that deserves a keenest attention. Yet, some spectators called it too tedious for the simple reason that speeches are not so interesting to them as gestures to which they are more accustomed. He also observes that the general makes a nice long speech just before he murders his loved wife, when, were one of us in his place, the boiling breast and the bursting heart would have actually struck the very tongue speechless. The quick-tempered Japanese race could never tolerate this: . . . such rhythmical, poetic speeches at such moments are only appreciated by the Westerners, whose emotional background is somewhat different from ours.

Another thing: the European tragedy is not terrible enough in some important points. Our spectators do not feel that any murder has been committed unless they are made to see the blood fly, flesh torn open, screams heard, and contortions and writhings take place generally. Desdemona's death is too easy. To be sure, there are the surroundings fitly suggestive of sadness, the lonely form in the white nightgown, the dark shadow of the dim lamp, and the stillness of the night exaggerated by the melancholy tone of the music. But what about the death itself? We are only permitted to hear one faint groan, scarcely audible, as Desdemona expires in her high bedchamber. This is, too, the last we see of her. To us, whose tears of sympathy are accustomed to fall generally upon the visible figure of the dead, this is a little too easy.

[The acting of Emilia made a tremendous impression on the Japanese audience. Her wild grief over the murder, her wild accusations directed at Othello, her condemnation of her husband, this devotion of waiting woman to mistress, seemed to impress the Japanese particularly.]

In this there was an unspeakable touch of reality and made us all feel that Emilia was, after all, the central character in this act rather than Othello or Iago.

Iago is the evil incarnate. There is no fixed aim in his

conduct except that he lives to do evil. . . . Evil is righteousness with him. He freely murders: he freely incites others to murder. Day in and day out the scheme to hurt someone is constantly on his mind. Takata Minoru was certainly the right person to act this part. His tallness and his thin whiskers even added much to his fitness to represent the character. [Mention is then made of his "detestable sickening smiles" and his "false tears."]

. . . Sada Yasco's personal charm and natural power to please added much to the brilliancy of the stage. Instead of the complex movements all that is required of Desdemona is to be gentle and obedient.

. . . She more than deserves our sympathy. But, in rashly running away from her father's house to wed her lover did she prove the gentleness of her character as a woman, though be it that the original drama is largely responsible for this?

. . . Othello's language, on the whole, is too rich. His words employed to relate the love affair existing between him and Desdemona at the council held in the prime minister's house are too poetical and unbecoming to the mouth of the coarse, sunburnt soldier that he is. The simple provincial language would have been much better. His speech before the murder, we repeat, is too unnatural and tedious. Had we got the rhythm of the language in which it was originally written, and had the taste of the spectators been more for speeches than for gestures it would have been proper enough. As it was, the charm was somewhat reduced.

However, there is a tremendous amount of courage in the actors' attempt to harmonize these strange elements with our national habit. With the exception of some details, they were eminently successful. The failure must be said to be largely due to the half-Japonized translation itself on which the play was based. This fact that the whole thing is the conglomeration of things European with things Japanese is shown by the keeping of the name of the play in its original form, *Othello*, while all the characters have been made over into Japanese.

Thus on ignorant English and Americans, and on cultivated Orientals, Shakespeare makes a deep impression. The Japanese criticism that Othello's language is "too rich," and their dislike of the famous speech at the council, which has been mouthed by every Anglo-Saxon schoolboy, is an objection — sometimes consciously, sometimes unconsciously felt by persons farther West. It is an objection based on the desire for realism in *language* as well as in psychology. Tolstoi's curious book on Shakespeare is written from the standpoint of a realistic novelist. Tolstoi declared that Shakespeare was not only not first class, he was not even second or third class; he is I think the only writer of reputation who has maintained that the original stories from which Shakespeare drew his plays are better than the plays themselves; and he selects as one of the worst dramas of Shakespeare, *King Lear*. Tolstoi said he had repeatedly tried to argue this matter with intelligent men, but such was their slavery to convention, they would not even discuss

THE TWENTIETH CENTURY THEATRE

the subject with him; that he had attempted to prove to Turgenev that Shakespeare was not a great writer, and Turgenev had refused to answer; he had merely turned sadly away. One reason why Tolstoi could not understand or appreciate Shakespeare was because of a certain perversity; he did not possess the blessed gift of admiration. He disliked to hear any famous author praised; and he loved to attack majority opinion. But there is more to it than this. He judged Shakespeare's speeches from the standpoint of realistic dialogue, and tried thus, they are of course absurd. A famous American actor once prophesied that soon Shakespeare would be banished from the stage, and that he deserved to be, because audiences would feel that his language was ridiculous.

It is certainly true that to-day if a college undergraduate should be told by his roommate that the latter had last night seen his dead father, and that, filled with curiosity, he should accompany his friend to the platform at midnight, and the ghost should appear, he would not speak a dozen lines of beautiful poetry,

"Angels and ministers of grace defend us!"

If he were able to say anything at all, he might exclaim

"*My God, it's father!!*"

THE TWENTIETH CENTURY THEATRE

Is Shakespeare right then, or wrong? Shakespeare is right. Neither Hamlet nor any other human being would recite poetry at a crisis, but Shakespeare was a poetic dramatist. The verse reveals, as no other diction could do, the exact condition of Hamlet's amazed and bewildered mind, with its thoughts beyond the reaches of his soul. Shakespeare's splendid poetry is there true to life in a more subtle way; he gives us the interpretation of Hamlet's thoughts. That realistic dramatist, Henry Arthur Jones, maintains that Shakespeare's language throughout his tragedies and comedies is at the bottom the purest realism.

Although Shakespeare is not acted in New York nearly so often as he ought to be, the tercentenary year 1916 is memorable. One hundred and thirty-nine performances of Shakespeare were given in the metropolis. The list was headed by *Hamlet*, which enjoyed thirty-five representations, owing principally to the presence of Forbes Robertson. John Drew acted thirty-three times in *Much Ado about Nothing*. *Othello*, given both by Forbes Robertson and by William Faversham, appeared twenty times; *The Merchant of Venice*, eighteen; *The Taming of the Shrew*, by both Julia Marlowe and Margaret Anglin, twelve; *As You Like It*, eight; *Macbeth*, with Sothern and Marlowe, five; *Romeo and Juliet*, four. A magnificent scenic production of *Macbeth* was given by James K. Hackett; and the most interesting revival of the year was *The Tempest*, produced by Louis Calvert and John Corbin, in which the former took the part of Prospero. Here one of my dreams was realised; tickets were sold to schoolchildren at reduced prices, and the matinée of *The Tempest* that I witnessed was graced by the presence of several hundred small boys and girls, whose delight I shall never forget.

In Germany in 1916 one hundred and fifty performances of Shakespeare were given, including twenty-three of his plays. One hundred and ninety theatres contributed to this result, and the list of pieces was headed by *A Midsummer Night's Dream*.

As the greatest dramatist in history was an Englishman, English-speaking people ought to have opportunities not only to see the chief plays frequently, but at some time or another to see them all. Of the thirty-seven dramas, I have witnessed twenty-seven. I hope before death I shall be able to reach completion, though I fear it will be a long time before I shall have a chance to see the three parts of *King Henry VI*. With all its coarseness, *Measure for Measure* is a good play on the stage; but I do not think Americans have had any opportunity to judge of this since the days of Madame Modjeska.

THE TWENTIETH CENTURY THEATRE

I shall have something to say about actors and acting in the next chapter; but there would surely be more enthusiasm for Shakespeare on the American stage if he were adequately presented. Great actors return to him again and again, unable to resist his fascination. But great actors are scarce. I remember sometime in the nineteenth century Richard Mansfield declaring with hot emphasis, that he would never, never act Shakespeare any more; yet not long after that renunciation, he produced *Henry V* followed by *Julius Cæsar*. We must have properly trained actors; dress models and matinée heroes are incapable. The proper reading of the lines — so that they shall be dramatically effective without losing their music — is very rare, and it may become a lost art. Here is where the actors of the "old school" shone to advantage, and we must go back to their methods. One of the best Shakespearean actors I ever heard was Milnes Levick, who used to appear with Margaret Mather. As *Macbeth*, he was not allowed to do his best, for he would have eclipsed the star; but as Mercutio, he was perfect. His rendition of the Queen Mab speech — one of the most severe tests on the stage — was marvellously effective.

There is at present no truly great actor who is identified with Shakespeare as Booth was with *Hamlet* or Salvini with *Othello*. Salvini's career covered an amazing span of years. Mrs. Browning, in a letter written in 1859, speaks enthusiastically of his acting, which she had just witnessed; thirty years later at one of his appearances in London, the *Times* said, "Conspicuous among the people in the stalls was Robert Browning, standing and waving his handkerchief during the recalls." At about the same period, I had the satisfaction of hearing his golden voice on the New York stage (I can hear it now); and he lived until the dawn of the tercentenary year, the first of January, 1916!

The greatest Cassius I ever saw was Lawrence Barrett. He was a charming man, cultivated, intelligent, full of amenity; he always did his best, and squandered money on expensive revivals; as Cassius he rose to greatness. The incomparable Edwin Booth was Brutus, but that particular night Cassius dominated the stage. It was a severe misfortune for Shakespearean productions in America that the New Theatre failed. Those who have been bored over and over again by stupid performances of Shakespeare, felt their hearts burn within them when the New Theatre company gave *Winter's Tale*. There was not a single dull moment; from beginning to end, the audience were thrilled. I am glad that Louis Calvert, who directed this presentation, has become an American citizen; and I only hope that his plans to produce a great many of Shakespeare's plays a great many times, may be realised.

The vacant throne of Shakespearean acting is evidenced by the rise of Robert Mantell. He pulled himself up from cheap and noisy melodrama by sheer industry, seeming to say that if no one else wanted to present the tragedies of Shakespeare, he would do it himself. And while the highest reaches of subtlety, poetry, and mystery are beyond his range, he deserves universal credit for giving hundreds and thousands of Americans opportunities to hear on the stage the words of the ever-living poet. He has given me my only opportunity to see *King John* and *King Lear;* and while no one has ever been completely successful in the rôle of Lear, much is to be learned from Mr. Mantell's interpretation; and his King John was adequate.

We know little of the personal character and opinions of William Shakespeare, but we do know his ideas about acting, of how an actor should comport himself on the stage, and how the actor should interpret his part. I believe that Shakespeare was really a better actor than he has the reputation of being. Ben Jonson, in his own edition of *Every Man in His Humour*, places his name high in the cast. I am certain he was not a great actor, in the sense that his contemporaries

THE TWENTIETH CENTURY THEATRE

Richard Burbage and Edward Alleyn were. Great actors find it difficult to teach others. They can neither explain nor transfer the secret of their art. But I believe that in Hamlet's speech to the players Shakespeare not only wrote out some of the fundamental principles of good acting but that he revealed something of his personal character. He evidently abhorred rant, exaggeration, playing to the gallery, merely theatrical effect; and he must have loved unaffected naturalness, the main feature of the art of Duse. Hamlet tells the players to be natural, to be sensible, to check momentary impulses, and never to be robustious. The voice of his creator is heard to the same effect when Hamlet declares that his affection for Horatio is because of the latter's self-control.

> Give me the man that is not passion's slave.

I remember the first time I ever heard the wonderful speech of Hamlet to his mother in the first act spoken by an intelligent actor, one who understood the significance of the language. It is no wonder that Claudius and Gertrude show toward the young prince a nervous hostility. He must have constantly got on their nerves. They were celebrating royal nuptials, men and women were in gay attire, there was feasting and merrymaking. In and out of the brilliant assemblage moved that sombre, silent, sable figure, a quiet but eloquent condemnation of everybody and everything. The Queen, apart from the disturbance caused by her conscience, was like many a mother with a brilliant son; she was a little afraid of him. In timidly rebuking him she happens to use the word "seems." Now the manner in which Hamlet replies is the first real test of the actor, and intelligent people in the audience know instantly whether he is good, ordinary, or bad. I have heard actors roar this speech, say it peevishly, interrupt it with sobs, do everything except speak the words like a gentleman. Never, I say, shall I forget the time when I first heard them spoken with sincerity and truth.

And I am ever hoping that I may live to that evening when some Cordelia will adequately make what I suppose is the greatest response among all the millions of responses in dramatic literature:

So young, and so untender? So young, my lord, and true.

But the fact is that for an ideal performance of Shakespeare, every part should be taken, not by a star — for this name covers a multitude of sins — but by a carefully trained and highly intelligent actor. The late Robert Ingersoll said that Shakespeare was so rich in thought and language that he gave away some of his most glorious speeches to fools, when any other author would have saved

THE TWENTIETH CENTURY THEATRE

them up for his best leading characters. In *Twelfth Night* it is the Clown who says:

> There is no darkness but ignorance.

This line alone would have made the reputation of any other writer, but Shakespeare in his prodigality carelessly tossed it into the mouth of a clown.

VI

ACTORS AND ACTING

Modern actors and acting — William Winter — influence of Ibsen — George Ade's satire — the Metropolitan Opera Company — Henry Irving in melodrama — Richard Mansfield — his ability — his services to the modern drama — Maude Adams — her presentation of works of genius — the growth of her ambition — Louis Calvert — his correspondence with Shaw — visits of foreign actors — two Russians — how long do actors and actresses live? — some statistics — art the great preservative.

IN the vitriolic attacks that the late William Winter made in the twilight of his life on the twentieth century theatre, which he continually minimised in comparison with the stage of his earlier days, it often seemed to me that he confused playwriting and playacting. Because there were no actors like Salvini, Irving, and Booth, he felt certain that the drama had degenerated. He was a scholarly, well-documented, experienced dramatic critic; his flag of idealism he never lowered, and finally abandoned his profession altogether rather than compromise. But somewhere around the year 1900, the gates of his mind closed. For the rest of his life he fed upon his memories, and as he had a richly-stored intellect, he got along with himself very well. Meanwhile the world advanced.

THE TWENTIETH CENTURY THEATRE

No wonder William Winter could not understand or appreciate the new drama, because he resolutely and steadily refused intellectual hospitality to Ibsen. Now whatever we may think of Ibsen's anarchistic and destructive social ideas, the mightiest influence on twentieth century drama in all countries is this Norwegian iconoclast. If, in Browning's language, we measure a mind's height by the shade it casts, Ibsen was a colossus. With the notable exception of Rostand, the influence of Ibsen is discernible on practically every important dramatist of to-day. The single fact that he, early in his career, elected to write plays rather than novels was potent in bringing about the coming supremacy of the drama. His revolutionary effect on the technique of modern drama is an inestimable blessing. He redeemed plot from artificiality, and dialogue from unreality. It is through the redemption of dialogue that has come the chief improvement in the modern theatre. He accomplished this supreme result; he compelled audiences to deserve their name; to hear plays rather than to see them, thus forcing dramatists to write for the ear rather than for the eye. The theatre had reached a condition where serious people seriously spoke of the spectators at the theatre and the audience at a ball game — with truth in both instances.

THE TWENTIETH CENTURY THEATRE

This new drama has not yet found among English-speaking actors as good interpreters as the romantic drama used to enjoy; and when William Winter indulged in his familiar denunciations of the modern theatre, he was really thinking of the good old days when the good old drama was presented by the good old stars — stars who were either born great or who achieved greatness, not stars that had greatness thrust upon them. I have no doubt also that he never could recapture his youthful delight in the theatre; alas, none of us can. I enjoy certain plays to-day that in my youth would have been quite beyond my range; I can only guess how that work of genius, *The Legend of Leonora*, would have passed over my head thirty years ago. But I am sure I shall never quite recapture the uncritical rapture of the days when I went to the theatre before seven o'clock, waited for the doors to open, paid twenty-five cents, raced with the mob up two flights of stairs to the top gallery, hurdled over the chairs at considerable risk to reach the first row, waited eagerly in a dark auditorium for an hour, watched then the lights go up, the blasé billionaires stroll to their reserved places in the orchestra chairs, heard the piano and fiddles, and finally entered into Paradise!

I feel certain that much of William Winter's bitterness came out of the vale of years.

But he was of course right in his lamentation over the decay of acting. Salvini, Booth, Irving, Mansfield, Jefferson (in his narrow field) are gone; and between their departure and the coming reign of the repertory actor, there is a confused interval where some of the stars are as far behind their advertisements as a patent medicine.

The idolised actors of the moving picture shows drew from our American humourist, George Ade, a delightfully burlesque but well-founded comparison between their methods and effects, and the art of the admirable William H. Crane. Here follows the speech made by Mr. Ade at a complimentary dinner given to Mr. Crane in 1916, and every sentence in it contains matter of mirth and matter for thought.

The Drama is roughly divided into Two parts — Tragedy and Comedy. Just Now it is more Roughly divided than Ever before.

According to all traditions of the Legitimate stage, the only Distinction between Tragedy and Comedy hinges on the Last Act.

In the good old days, if most of the principals curled up and Died in the last act, the play was a Tragedy. If they stood in a line and Bowed, the play was a Comedy.

Our guest of Honour and You, gentlemen, can recall the time when a Play in which some one was Shot, Stabbed, Assaulted and Battered, and left Unconscious at Centre was a genuine Tragedy, entitled to come under the Observation of William Winter.

THE TWENTIETH CENTURY THEATRE

Thanks to the Southern California School of Art all that has been Changed. Nowadays, when the Hero is Shot, the Play-house resounds with Shrieks of Laughter.

When he is struck on the head with some Blunt Instrument and falls Unconscious the Large Lady seated Next to you goes into a Paroxysm of Mirth.

If he is seen to disappear beneath the Waves, with Bubbles arising to mark the spot at which he sank, the Film Exchanges announce that the Comedy is Sure Fire.

Mr. Crane can remember when the Comedian received his training in the Library. Now he gets it in the Gymnasium. He can remember when Comedy was a Dramatic Treatment of Conflicting Purposes, with a Happy Ending.

He can recall a Later period in which Comedy was anything that would make them Laugh.

I am Wondering if he can revise some of his Quaint Old-fashioned Notions and accept the New dictum that Comedy has its headquarters Below the Waist-line.

However, we are not here to Brood over the Degeneracy of the times.

Doubtless it is True that the Drama is having more things Done to it at present than Ever before.

Real Tragedy is found Only in the New York Offices of the Producing Managers.

The most Serious contributions to Current Theatrical History are the Statements from the One-night Stands.

Thespis has temporarily stood aside to make room for St. Vitus.

The gentleman who could not write Home for Money Five Years Ago is now writing Scenarios.

The delirium seems to be at the most Acute Stage — temperature about 104. When the fever Breaks, the Patient

THE TWENTIETH CENTURY THEATRE

is going to be very Weak, but probably he will be out of Danger.

And so, in these times, when there are more Theatres than Delicatessen Shops and all you have to Do to be an Actor is to have your picture Taken, it is well to be Philosophical, knowing that Art is Long and Salary-Contracts are Short.

At the risk of repeating what All the other speakers may say, I wish to assure Mr. Crane that He is respected by the men who try to write for the stage because he has Stood for Reputable Plays. He has proceeded upon the Theory that the Patrons of the Drama live at Home with their Own Families.

He has stood for Home-Grown Plays of the Kind that strengthen the Self-respect of Americans.

I know what Mr. Crane has Stood For, because I have written two Plays for him.

It is because he is the spokesman of True Comedy and was the friend of the American play when it didn't have a Friend in the House that we are here to give him our Verbal Bouquets.

Those of us who are more than fifty years of age I count fortunate, for we have vivid memories of men and women on the stage whose peers do not exist to-day. In the opera, I suppose that neither before and certainly not since has there ever been a collection of singers equal to the Metropolitan Company in the early nineties, under the direction of Maurice Grau. The cast for *Faust* was advertised as the "ideal cast"; and it really was, for it is

THE TWENTIETH CENTURY THEATRE

impossible to imagine how an opera could be more perfectly given than *Faust* was by Jean and Edouard De Reszké, Lassalle, Scalchi, Bauermeister, and Emma Eames. In the eighties, those of us who heard Wagner interpreted by Alvary and Lilli Lehmann went away absolutely content. It was a fine thing for America that New York possessed for the whole winter — and for season after season — the foremost operatic company in the world. And although America has produced very few great men singers, America has given to the world more great women singers in the last twenty-five years than those supplied by any other nation.

In the theatre, we had actors who also equalled their fame. Booth must have been at his best in the seventies, before I heard him; for in the eighties although I went again and again, he only once rose to the supreme heights — that was one night in Detroit, when he appeared as Shylock. (I have always regretted that I never saw him in *The Fool's Revenge*.) Irving was of course in the plenitude of his powers, but I thought him greater in melodrama than in Shakespeare. He was never satisfactory to me as Shylock or Macbeth; but in *The Bells, Louis XI*, and especially in *The Lyons Mail*, he was overwhelming. I would go so far as to say that those who never saw Irving in one or more of these three rôles, never saw the real Irving at all.

tion in a star is often a ruinous thing for her managers or supporters; by that sin fell the "angels" not once, but many times. No actor is more ambitious than Maude Adams; she would rather miss the heights occasionally in the finest plays than triumph in those on a lower scale. It is worth remembering that for a number of years she has appeared only in the plays of the two men who are respectively the first living dramatists of France and Great Britain — Rostand and Barrie. It is owing to her that we had in America the opportunity of hearing in English *L'Aiglon* and *Chantecler;* and although the critics were acidulous because of her audacity in putting on the latter play, for the leading rôle of which she was conspicuously unfitted physically, it is probable that if it had not been for her courage, we should not have seen *Chantecler* at all, and it would have been a misfortune to have lived without it. Whatever may be said of her lack of physique in this rôle, the audience followed from beginning to end with tense interest, and I thought it altogether the most impressive play and performance of that season. She interprets the subtle, charming, and profound character-studies of J. M. Barrie with consummate skill. She is a public benefactor, and I wish she could live forever; she has developed steadily since her first season with *The Little Minister*, and audiences know in going to the theatre where she appears, they will see not only a fascinating woman, but the best play of the year.

I wish that every actor and every theatre-goer in America would read *Problems of the Actor*, by Louis Calvert, published in 1918. Mr. Calvert was one of the most accomplished members of the New Theatre company; no one will forget his interpretation of old Anthony, in John Galsworthy's *Strife*. Since the demise of that organisation, he has appeared in various rôles, the most important of which is Andrew Undershaft, in *Major Barbara*. He has now become an American citizen, and hopes eventually to produce many plays of Shakespeare. No one knows better than he the evils of both the star system and the fashion of long runs. Both are incompatible with anything resembling a national theatre. If we had a national theatre, Mr. Calvert's position in it would be very much like that of Féraudy in the Comédie Française; for both M. Féraudy and Mr. Calvert are thoroughly competent artists in all varieties of tragic and comic effect. Both have been trained in the most intelligent manner, that is to say, in a good stock repertory company. Mr. Calvert was brought up in the Manchester theatre, and learned his art by appearing in classic and modern plays. In this new book, he discourses in a clear, forceful, and entertaining manner of the fundamental things in good acting. He believes the actor must begin at the bottom, and work up, paying attention to the mastery of every detail. Furthermore, he believes that the play is the thing, and that the business of the actor is to interpret it. But he speaks not only of acting, but of everything connected with the presentation; that is to say, of scenery, costume, lighting, music, and in fact, of all necessities. Every actor, young or old, will learn something from this book, because it comes out of long and successful experience; and every play-goer will advance through these pages toward becoming what every play-goer should become—an intelligent critic.

In 1905, when *Major Barbara* had its first performance in England, Bernard Shaw, who knew well enough the real capacity of Louis Calvert, hoped to sting him into superhuman efforts by the following letter:

> Derry, Rosscarbery, Co. Cork,
> 23d July, 1905.

Dear Calvert: Can you play the trombone? If not, I beg you to acquire a smattering of the art during your holidays. I am getting on with the new play, scrap by scrap, and the part of the millionaire cannon founder is becoming more and more formidable. Broadbent and Veegan rolled into one, with Mephistopheles thrown in: that is what it is like. "Business is Business" will be cheap melodrama in comparison. Irving and Tree will fade into the third class when Calvert takes the stage as Andrew Undershaft. It will be TREMENDOUS, simply. But there is a great scene at the end of the second act where he buys up the Salvation Army, and has to take part in a march to a big meeting. Barker will play the drum. You will have a trombone — or bombardon if you prefer that instrument — and it would add greatly to the effect if you could play it prettily. Besides, if you took to music you could give up those confounded cigars and save your voice and your memory (both wrecks, like Mario's, from thirty-seven cigars a day) for this immense part. It is very long — speeches longer than Keegan's and dozens of them, and infinite nuances of execution. Undershaft is diabolically subtle, gentle, self-possessed, powerful, stupendous, as well as amusing and interesting. There are the makings of ten Hamlets and six Othellos in his mere leavings. Learning it will half kill you, but you can retire next day as pre-eminent and unapproachable. That penny-plain and two-pence-coloured pirate Brassbound will be beneath your notice then. I have put him off for another year, as I cannot get the right Lady Cicely. Vedrenne, unluckily, has read my plays at Margate, and is now full of the most insane proposals — wants Brassbound instantly with you and Kate Rorke, for one thing.

But the trombone is the urgent matter of the moment. By the way, trombone players never get cholera nor consumption — never die, in fact, until extreme old age makes them incapable of working the slide.

G. BERNARD SHAW.

After the first performance, Mr. Shaw wrote the actor this delightful epistle:

THE TWENTIETH CENTURY THEATRE

10 Adelphi Terrace, W. C.

My dear Calvert:

I see with disgust that the papers all say that your Undershaft was a magnificent piece of acting, and "Major Barbara" a rottenly undramatic play, instead of pointing out that "Major Barbara" is a masterpiece and you the most infamous amateur that ever disgraced the boards.

Do let me put Cremlin into it. A man who could let the seven deadly sins go for nothing could sit on a hat without making an audience laugh. I have taken a box for Friday and had a hundredweight of cabbages, dead cats, eggs, and gingerbeer bottles stacked in it. Every word you fluff, every speech you *unact*, I will shy something at you. Before you go on the stage I will insult you until your temper gets the better of your lines. You are an impostor, a sluggard, a blockhead, a shirk, a malingerer, and the worst actor that ever lived or ever will live. I will apologise to the public for engaging you: I will tell your mother of you. Barker played you off the stage; Cremlin dwarfed you; Bill annihilated you; Clare Greet took all eyes from you. If you do not recover yourself next time, a thunderbolt will end you. If you are too lazy to study the lines, I'll coach you in them. That last act MUST be saved, or I'll withdraw the play and cut you off with a shilling.
Yours ever. G. B. S.[1]

The reason why a stock company is so much finer a school for actors than any other stage-experience, is because in a stock company every actor on the stage is acting all the time whether he is at the moment entrusted with a speech or not.

[1] These letters appeared in the New York *Times*.

THE TWENTIETH CENTURY THEATRE

Mr. Calderon, in his acute criticism of Chekhov's plays as produced at the Artistic Theatre in Moscow, observes that every member of the cast is busy, and compares the situation to that of the English stage, where while the star is speaking, the rest of the company resemble that "pathetic little group" of players surrounding a golf tee, paralysed with awe-struck immobility.

When foreign actors who have been properly trained in a repertory theatre come to America, whether they speak the lines in a native or a strange tongue, they often produce a powerful effect on intelligent audiences. I remember a competent French actress of no particular fame in Europe, who presented in New Haven Bernstein's play *The Whirlwind* (*La Rafale*) in English; her faulty accent did not prevent her from thrilling us all. When Madame Nazimova first came to this country with Orlenev, I heard their performance of *The Master Builder* in Russian; and although the spoken words were quite unintelligible to me, the play most emphatically "got over." Later Madame Nazimova learned English, and presented *Hedda Gabler* in a manner that for the first time made this drama transparently clear. Her success has not been an unmitigated blessing. She has since acquired some mannerisms. But before her early training had become frayed, she was wonderful. I have seen Ibsen's plays spoken in English, French, and German; but altogether the most impressive production was that given in America and in the Russian language by Madame Komisarzhevskaia, the only actress who completely convinced me that the Nora of the last act had naturally developed out of the "little squirrel" of the first. Her acting was particularly remarkable for its reserve and restraint; she was free from all theatrical tricks. In America she was eager to appear in *Sister Beatrice*, her favourite play, and how I wish she might have done so! But to her complete bewilderment, she discovered that somebody or other had the exclusive "rights." Later she became a martyr to her art; after her return to Russia, having promised to act in a province where there was an epidemic of smallpox, she insisted on keeping her engagement, although implored by her home-friends not to do so; she caught the disease, and was followed to her grave by thousands of weeping Russians. I have never seen either on or off the stage a woman of more quiet dignity; and I shall forget neither her acting nor the gracious modesty in which she spoke in conversation of her ideals.

Bernard Shaw jocosely recommended Louis Calvert to learn the trombone because trombone-playing ministered to longevity. In the first chapter of this book, I called attention to the elevation both in moral character and social position of the actors in a resident stock company as compared to barnstormers. It may not seem to anyone but the actor himself to be a matter of importance, but I believe that the resident actor in a repertory theatre will certainly live longer as well as more happily than the subordinate player on the road. Here follow some statistics collected by one of my pupils, Mr. W. S. Hunt, which throw light on the average longevity of actors. I do not have an absolute faith in figures of this kind, but so far as they go, they are valuable. These numbers begin with English-born actors who were born as far back as 1725, and continue to those who have lived to the year 1900.

Average longevity of all actors . . . . . . 55 years
Average longevity of all actresses . . . . . 52 years
Average longevity of the Star Actor . . . . 66.8 years
Average longevity of the ordinary actor . . . 45 years
Average longevity of the Star Actress . . . 61.2 years
Average longevity of the ordinary actress . . 37.3 years

The "ordinary actress" includes chorus girls.

It will be observed that the star actor lives twenty-one years longer than the ordinary actor; the star actress nearly twenty-four years longer than the ordinary actress. Perhaps this last discrepancy reveals the conditions of life for the women who do not reach the top.

THE TWENTIETH CENTURY THEATRE

Comparing the lives of eighteenth century actors with those of the nineteenth, there appears to be a difference of only about two years in favour of the nineteenth. This with improved theatres, more sanitary conditions, better aired dressing-rooms, etc.

So far as statistics will bear out the statement, the first generation of actors is longer-lived than the second by about seven years.

In the above average longevities the level was raised by the great age of C. Kemble, W. Betty, Macready, Braham, and C. Macklin of whom one account says that he played for sixty-five years, and lived to the age of one hundred and two. The level was somewhat depressed by Adelaide Neilson, who died at thirty-two, and Edmund Kean, who died at forty-five.

Not only will the properly trained repertory actor live longer than the ordinary actor of to-day, but he will certainly have for a longer time the delight of activity in his profession. In a recent number of the *Manchester Guardian*, there is an interesting article on *The Stage at Seventy*. After commenting on the decline in the art of acting, the writer says, "The question is not whether you can act but whether you are popular. And as popularity is perishable goods the actor now lasts no longer than a fast bowler, and the actress perhaps not so long. . . . With the ladies the case is worse. They rely mainly on their beauty, which, unlike humour, does not endure, and unlike art, does not increase with years. As between incompetents twenty-one will beat thirty-one almost every time."

VII

DRAMATIC CRITICISM

The standards of dramatic criticism — freedom of the critic — sincerity — some good dramatic critics in America — is theatrical criticism an art, or is it news? — fatal effects of the morning after — the manager and the critic — the actor and the critic — monthly criticisms — zest for the theatre.

ALMOST as important as the elevation of the art of acting and of the social position of the actor is the elevation of the standards of dramatic criticism. The public does not care very much what the newspaper critics say, because of the general suspicion that they are not allowed to say what they think. There should of course be no connexion between the press agent, the advertiser, and the dramatic critic. Let the press agent lay it on with a trowel; let the advertisement flare; but let the critic say what he conceives to be the truth. The New York *Times* had the courage to fight this matter out with the managers, and the *Times* won. But without detracting one iota from the courage of the *Times*, that great newspaper had something in addition to courage; it had capital, a very present help to freedom of opinion. It has often

THE TWENTIETH CENTURY THEATRE

been stated — I do not know how truly — that most newspapers cannot afford through adverse criticisms published in their columns to run the risk of losing the theatre advertisements. This is not a condition peculiar to America. In 1912 I was informed by a theatre-director in Munich that the same unfortunate condition prevailed all over the German empire. But there was then a corrective in Germany; the first-night audience. Whatever the critics might be restrained from saying was said by the audience in no uncertain tone. No matter how high the reputation of the actors, no matter how strong their hold on public affection, if the play was bad, the audience hissed or gave vent to their feelings in roars of derisive laughter. I have repeatedly seen famous and beloved actors and actresses hissed off the stage simply because the play was flimsy or absurd. And the actors understood it was not their fault.

A great dramatic critic with a free hand might have a powerful influence on the American stage. Nothing perhaps is more difficult than to win lasting fame in the field of literary or dramatic criticism. But it is not impossible. Lessing, Hazlitt, Sainte-Beuve, Sarcey, Arnold, Bielinski, Herzen, have had a real effect on the course of literature and drama. If the New Theatre had arranged that one high-class critic should write authoritative reviews of each new production, the result would have been salutary.

The dramatic criticisms that appear in most of our newspapers certainly do not reflect anything more than the average intelligence of the audience. And if one reads many newspapers outside of our large centres of population, as I do, one must believe that the majority of dramatic criticisms published in them are as timid as they are undiscriminating. It is not very often that one finds a combination of sincerity and cerebration. I remember reading with agreeable surprise the following article — remarkable only for candour — in a Hartford newspaper, in March, 1903: "The settings and costumes were elaborate and the audiences were well pleased, applause and laughter being the rule. The price charged for the best seats in the house, two dollars, seems large for a play of the kind presented, but if people are willing to pay that amount there is no reason why the management will not charge it. It is a fact, however, that early in October, 1901, *The Altar of Friendship* was given a much better production by John Mason and his companions and that the house was but partly filled at that time, though the scale of prices was much lower." This brief criticism was refreshing for two things; its refusal to surrender to bad acting, and its ability to refer to something better in the past.

So much of the work of play-notices is handed over to reporters or to journalistic birds of passage, that neither standards nor background can be expected.

Outside of professional circles, I suppose men rarely buy a newspaper to see what the dramatic critic says of such and such a performance; but if we had more critics of wit, of intelligence, of intrepid honesty, I think the circulation of newspapers might be increased by them, just as many a newspaper has had a large addition made to its subscription list by the regular contributions of a good professional humourist or cartoonist.

In the autumn of 1908, one journal in New York attacked another, distinctly saying that a critic had been dismissed because his writings offended the managers, and his employers felt that they could not afford to lose the advertisements. The journal thus attacked immediately brought suit for libel. I regret that this case never came up in the courts, for it would have given the public an opportunity to learn the truth. It may be that the attack was unfair and that the resulting general suspicion was groundless; but a general suspicion on matters of literary integrity is a good thing for nobody, and the whole subject ought to have been made clear.

There are in America a number of excellent dramatic critics, men who are well equipped in scholarship, in knowledge of the modern drama in both

THE TWENTIETH CENTURY THEATRE

Europe and America, and who know how to write penetrating and luminous criticism; such men as Walter P. Eaton, James S. Metcalfe, John Corbin, Acton Davies, James Huneker, George J. Nathan, J. R. Towse, Clayton Hamilton, H. T. Parker, by no means exhaust the list; they have done good service, and are capable of doing more. For some reason, the trained musical critics seem to have a freer hand in adverse criticism than their brothers in the field of drama. W. J. Henderson, H. T. Finck, H. E. Krehbiel, Max Smith, and others have no restraint of any kind, if we can judge by the opposition they arouse. It is the common belief that more special knowledge and training are required for the position of musical than for dramatic critic; possibly therefore these gentlemen feel the security that comes from recognition as an expert authority.

An excellent English dramatic critic told me that he often fell asleep during the first night of a play; and upon my naïvely asking, "Aren't you afraid the author will see you?" he replied, "If he did, he would be the last person to mention it."

There is one reform that seems to me to be essential if we are to have authoritative dramatic criticism. *The critic should not be forced to write his article the same night of a play, nor should it ever appear on the morning after.* As a matter of common fairness to the playwright and to the theatrical manager, the critic should be allowed sufficient time for adequate reflection and composition. The dramatist may have spent two years of hard labour on his piece; the manager has spent much money; the actors may have been carefully drilled; and the critic is expected to put into the impressively permanent form of type a judgment on the whole production instantaneously formed and written in feverish haste. One New York critic told me that he always wrote his criticisms on the elevated train running from near the theatre to the office of the newspaper. He who runs may read; but he who runs cannot write. This seems grotesquely unfair to those who have spent so much time and effort in preparation, and to whom success or failure is vital.

It is as absurd to expect a competent criticism the morning after the first night as it would be to insist that a book-review should appear the day after publication. Indeed the latter would be more reasonable; for at all events the literary critic would have the book before his eyes in cold type.

This evil custom of the morning-after arises from the common notion that dramatic criticism is not an art, but "news"; and that therefore the sooner it appears the better. Now the morning after a first night, there should be in the newspaper a brief and accurate account of what actually happened at the theatre. The name of play and author; the principal actors; the kind of play; its reception by the audience. Criticism should be reserved for the day following or for the Sunday Supplement.

I have not seen the slightest allusion to the following fact, but I feel like paying a tribute for it to the New York *Tribune*. During the last two years, the *Tribune* has contained no criticism of a new play until two days after the performance. So far as I know, this is the only American newspaper that has adopted this custom.

In Paris, a *répétition générale* precedes the first night. No tickets are sold for this dress rehearsal, but all the critics are invited. The next day comes the *première*, when the critic may go again if he wishes; his review is not published until the day after the *première*, and detailed criticism is even then customarily reserved until the Sunday issue. Winthrop Ames adopted this idea at the Little Theatre; an audience that filled the house was invited to attend the dress rehearsal, for it is impossible to judge correctly of the value of a play unless a real audience is present; then came the *première*. Unfortunately for his plan, nearly all the newspapers published their criticisms of the play the morning after the dress rehearsal, seeming to be afraid that some other papers might get ahead of them.

THE TWENTIETH CENTURY THEATRE

Our metropolitan Sunday papers have for some years past endeavoured to correct the evil of snapshot judgment by printing two pages about the local theatres, wherein the critic has an opportunity to correct himself, revise his opinions, and treat important plays in the lengthy and detailed manner they deserve. Many of these articles are exceedingly valuable to students of contemporary drama. The *Tribune* is the only daily paper that attempts to classify current productions in a weekly list; while hundreds of the floating population in New York, who constitute of course the majority of the audiences, consult the excellent and pungent "guide" provided in every number of *Life* by the accomplished veteran, Metcalfe.

The ordinary manager hates the critic, and in many cases wishes that all dramatic criticism could be abolished. Even if the manager can to any extent control the criticism in the newspaper, he does not like the job, for it gives him no end of trouble; but he knows that adverse criticism really hurts his business, and causes almost hysterical distress in his company of players, many of whom have to be soothed and stroked before they feel like going on. To him the critic is a constant nuisance. But I believe that if criticism could be properly deferred, could always be honest and intelligent, and whether adverse or favourable, could be constructive — mere denunciation, sarcasm, or gush, replaced by something aidful — the fair-minded manager might come to look upon the critic as a valuable ally.

Actors and actresses are hair-trigger sensitive, as are all people who live by public favour; even the great Lessing in the eighteenth century was forced to abandon criticisms of the performers, after a few visits from irate actresses. As a rule, even this kind of adverse comment might be made more helpful than it sometimes is; though there are occasions when simple annihilation is the only way. I remember in a column review of Tree's *Hamlet* in the New York *Sun*, one sentence was devoted to Mrs. Tree. "Mrs. Tree played Ophelia; and she should never do it again." And at one outrageous presentation of a great Continental drama, the *Sun* critic closed his review by the remark, "The players threaten to repeat the performance to-morrow night."

But I insist that all criticism, both praise and blame, ought to be so constructive that it will help not only the prospective theatre-goer, but the dramatist, manager, and actors. It is easy enough to score off a bad performance by holding it up to public ridicule; but what real advantage is gained by this? We read a display of the critic's ironical powers with a laugh, and then straightway forget all about it; but the unfortunate actor or actress is sleepless with writhing agony. As the critic whets his beak, let him realise the probable effect of his words; then if he is certain that ultimate good will result from castigation, let him bite, backed by brains and conscience. And of course, in most cases, sincere condemnation is more fruitful than unintelligent praise.

Another thing. I have often taken up a metropolitan journal to see what the dramatic critic says of a new play, and finding a column and a half, begun to read with eagerness, only to discover that three-quarters of the "criticism" is a detailed account of the plot of the piece. This seems to me worse than superfluous. When I go to a new play, I never want to know the story in advance; half the pleasure is in watching the fable develop; and one cannot nearly so well judge of the playwright's skill if one knows beforehand all the climaxes. I suspect the only reason why so many critics take up the major space of their articles with retelling the plot, is because they have not a sufficient number of ideas to fill a column with real criticism. That is the inference I invariably draw.

Owing to the unsatisfactory nature of hasty newspaper dramatic reviews, which fail to satisfy the growing army of Americans who take a serious interest in the theatre, many monthly magazines now employ a trained critic to discuss contemporary productions. Some of the most thoughtful essays on the modern drama may be found in these periodicals. Mr. Lawrence Gilman, in the *North American Review*, who is a literary, musical, and dramatic critic, often supplies an article worth preservation. Clayton Hamilton serves with equal usefulness on the staff of *The Bookman*. A sign of the times is the fact that only recently has the New York *Nation* devoted a regular department to the drama.

Best of all, every year sees more and more amateur critics in American audiences; men and women who know the difference between good and bad plays, between good and bad acting, persons who cannot be deceived by counterfeit coin. If all audiences were intelligent and discriminating, the millennium of the drama would materialise. Everyone who has made even an elementary study of the art of the theatre knows how enormously his delight in a good performance is increased by knowledge. It is a pity that so many theatre-goers witness a play so ignorantly; they look on at a play as a man would regard a game of chess who did not know the difference between a pawn and a knight. But so soon as one *understands*, so soon as one sees the mind of the dramatist interpreted by subtle acting, one enjoys pure happiness. Men and women ought to take dramatic art seriously if

THE TWENTIETH CENTURY THEATRE

for no other reason than to add to the pleasure of existence.

And what happiness the theatre gives us! Some of the happiest afternoons and evenings of my life have been passed in witnessing plays — pure, flawless delight that remains as a permanent addition to memory. The theatre is one of the greatest blessings of humanity, and I feel an unpayable debt of gratitude to the dramatists, the managers, and the long list of actors and actresses who have by their efforts given me so much pleasure. Nor shall I ever become sufficiently sophisticated to lose the keen anticipation of a night at the play. I am not ashamed to confess that I love the preliminary moments, the crowded house of men and women, who have left their troubles somewhere else; the lights and the proleptic music; the sudden darkness; the ascent of the curtain — these will thrill me to my last hour on earth.

Of all the pages of Addison, I like most the description of Sir Roger at the play. "As soon as the house was full, and the candles lighted, my old friend stood up and looked about him with that pleasure which a mind seasoned with humanity naturally feels in itself at the sight of a multitude of people who seem pleased with one another, and partake of the same common entertainment."

POSTSCRIPT

ROSTAND AND FRANCE

FOR many centuries to come the word *France* will be a word full of glory and honour, and all those who have French blood in their veins will be glad of it. The heroic sacrifices made by France and the French people, since the invaders occupied their soil in 1914, have awakened the lasting admiration of the whole world. The Germans, in an attempt to destroy France, have raised her to the highest pinnacle of splendour.

I believe that the personality of Edmond Rostand and the spirit of his great dramas have had no small influence on the modern French mind, and I believe that they have been an inspiration to the French soldiers and women in this war. The spirit of all has been the spirit exhibited by Cyrano. The Parisian attitude of skepticism, cynicism, and mockery, characteristic of a certain group of writers in Paris before 1914, has been transformed into a spirit of heroism. I remember reading an article by a French critic in 1912, who said that nowadays the only attitude possible toward the so-called great problems of life was a Smile. This attitude has ever been detestable to Rostand, and his plays, poems, and speeches have been a conscious protest against it. When he was elected to the French Academy, his address, delivered on the fourth of June, 1903, was a call to arms — a call for a spiritual awakening. He meant to make Idealism respectable, and not only respectable, but fashionable. In this memorable speech we find the following words: "The poison of to-day, which we have no longer the right to dose people with, is the delicious essence which stupefies conviction and kills energy. We must restore passion. And even emotion, which is not absurd. We must remind these timid Frenchmen who are always afraid of not being sufficiently ironical, that there can be plenty of modern cleverness in a resolute eye."

France has shown this marvellous spirit since the year 1914. It is a remarkable fact that *Cyrano de Bergerac*, which I believe to be the greatest drama of the modern period, has been also an unspeakably stimulating and ennobling force.

INDEX

Achelis, T., 86.
Adams, M., her career, 119, 120.
Addison, J., Sir Roger at the play, 141.
Ade, G., his speech on acting, 114–116.
Ames, W., Little Theatre, 21, 136.
Andreev, L., 5.
Anglin, M., 103.
Anspacher, L., *The Unchastened Woman*, 5, 18, 59.
Antoine, A., Paris director, 76, 77.
Archer, W., comment on American and British stage, 60, 66; translation of Ibsen, 85.

Bahr, H., 5.
Baker, G. P., his Harvard course, 83, 84.
Barker, G., 5; his New York productions, 21, 44, 59, 92.
Barrett, L., his Cassius, 106.
Barrett, W., 96.
Barrie, J. M., 5, 7; publishing plays, 8; *What Every Woman Knows*, 14; *The Old Lady Shows Her Medals*, 40; *The Twelve Pound Look*, 63; *Leonora*, 113; *Little Minister*, 120.
Barrymore, L., his acting, 59.
Becque, H., 77, 83.
Bennett, A., 7, 72.
Bernhardt, S., 118.
Björnson, B., 4.
Booth, E., 105, 106, 117.
Browne, M., Chicago Little Theatre, 77, 78.
Browning, E. B., remark on Salvini, 106.
Browning, R., 90, 106, 112.
Burton, R., *Rahab*, 89.

Caine, H., dramatising novels, 54.
Calderon, G., criticism of Chekhov, 125.
Calvert, L., his services, 21, 22; production of *Tempest*, 104; of *Winter's Tale*, 106; his book, 121; relations with Shaw, 121–124.
Chekhov, A., 5, 7; *Cherry Orchard*, 26; Calderon's remark on, 125.
Cohan, G. M., his advance, 73, 74.
Coquelin, C., 118.
Corbin, J., 134; production of *Tempest*, 22, 104; remarks on *Herod*, 91.
Corelli, M., 56.
Cournos, J., article on Craig, 45.
Craig, G., his ideas on scenery, 44, 45.
Crane, W. H., Ade's tribute to, 114, 115.
Crawford, J., work at Dartmouth, 84.
Crocker, C. T., 86.

Daly, A., his company, 18.
D'Annunzio, G., 5.
Davies, A., 134.
Dillingham, C., the Hippodrome, 38.
Dreiser, T., his plays, 79, 80.
Drew, J., 103.
Dryden, J., his prefaces, 10.
Duse, E., 108, 118.

Eaton, W. P., 134.
Eliot, S. A., Indianapolis Little Theatre, 79.
Euripides, 64.

Faversham, W., 91, 103.
Féraudy, M., 121.

INDEX

Finck, H. T., 134.
Fiske, M. M., 53, 88.
Fitch, C., founder of American drama, 5; *The Truth*, 60.
Fitzsimmons, R., his acting, 57.
Forbes-Robertson, J., 75, 103.
Frohman, D., his work for the theatre, 18.

Galsworthy, J., 5, 7; *Justice*, 16, 18, 80; *Strife*, 121.
George, G., her stock company, 18, 21, 22.
Gilman, L., his critics, 140.
Glaspell, S., *Trifles*, 78.
Goodman, J., 84.
Gorki, M., 5, 7.
Greet, B., production of *Everyman*, 88; recent Shakespeare productions, 97.

Hackett, J. K., production of *Macbeth*, 104.
Hamilton, C., his critical work, 134, 140.
Hardwick, J. B., her ballad on dramatised novels, 55.
Hardy, T., *The Dynasts*, 5, 92.
Hauptmann, G., 5, 7; *Weavers* in English, 18.
Henderson, W. J., 134.
Herbert, V., *Eileen*, 41.
Heyse, P., 88.
Hofmannsthal, H., 5.
Holt, R., speech on the drama, 81, 82.
Hopkins, A., director, 37.
Hopkins, C., director, 86.
Horniman, A. E. F., her Manchester company, 25.
Housum, R., *The Gipsy Trail*, 37.
Howard, B., his prophecy, 6.
Huneker, J., 134.
Hunt, W. S., statistics on the longevity of actors, 127.

Ibsen, H., 4; his influence, 112; Russian actresses of, 125, 126.

Ingersoll, R., remark on Shakespeare, 109.
Irving, H., best in melodrama, 117.

James, H., remark on printing plays, 8.
Jefferson, J., 118, 119.
Jones, H. A., 5; publication of plays, 9; prefaces, 10; remark on Shakespeare, 103.
Jonson, B., attack on Elizabethan drama, 2-4; prefaces, 10; *Silent Woman*, 83; mention of Shakespeare as an actor, 107.

Keene, T. W., 94.
Knoblauch, E., 84.
Komisarzhevskaia, her acting of Ibsen, 126.
Krehbiel, H., 134.

Lemaître, J., remark on Antoine's experiment, 76.
Lessing, G. E., 138.
Levick, M., acting of Mercutio, 105.
Lyman, E., founder of the Northampton theatre, 75.

Mackay, C., her book on Little Theatres, 74-77.
Maeterlinck, M., 4; *Blue Bird*, 26; *Mary Magdalene*, 88.
Mansfield, R., Shakespeare productions, 95, 104; his career, 118, 119.
Mantell, R., his rise, 107.
Marlowe, J., 103.
Masefield, J., 89.
Mather, M., 105.
Mathison, E. W., 89.
Metcalfe, J. S., criticisms, 134, 137.
Miln, G. C., acting Hamlet, 94.
Modjeska, H., 104.
Moody, W. V., 5, 7.

Nathan, G. J., 134.
Nazimova, A., 125, 126.

INDEX

Opp, J., appearance in *Herod*, 9.

Parker, H. T., 134.
Parker, L. N., 89.
Parry, M., 86.
Peabody, J. P., 84, 90.
Phillips, S., 5, 7; *Herod*, 89, 91, 92.
Pinero, A. W., 5, 72.
Poli, S., his New Haven stock company, 22, 23.

Rea, J., allusion to Jonson, 3.
Rostand, E., 4, 112; *La Samaritaine*, 88; *Cyrano*, 119, 144; *Chantecler*, 120; his influence on the French war spirit, 143, 144.

Salvini, T., 105, 106.
Sargent, F., his services, 82, 83.
Sayler, O. M., article on *Laughing Gas*, 80.
Schnitzler, A., 5.
Shakespeare, W., remarks on acting, 107, 108; *Tempest*, 22, 104; *Titus Andronicus*, 93; *Macbeth*, 94, 103–105; *Hamlet*, 94–96, 103, 105, 107, 108; *Julius Cæsar*, 95, 105, 106; *Romeo and Juliet*, 96, 103; *Othello*, Japanese performance of, 97–101, 103, 105; *Lear*, 101, 107, 109; *Much Ado*, 103; *Merchant of Venice*, 103, 117; *As You Like It*, 103; *Taming of the Shrew*, 103; *Measure for Measure*, 104; *Henry V*, 105; *Winter's Tale*, 106; *Antony and Cleopatra*, 20; *King John*, 107; *Twelfth Night*, 110; *Richard III*, 118.
Sharp, W., prophecy on the drama, 5.
Shaw, G. B., 5, 7; prefaces, 10, 11; *Major Barbara*, 18, 122–124; remark on beginning performances, 62; *Androcles*, 90; relations with Calvert, 122–124.
Sheldon, E., 84.
Smith, M., 134.
Sothern, E., 53, 95, 103.
Stanislavski, his Artistic Theatre, 26.
Steele, R., attack on contemporary stage, 4.
Strindberg, A., 4.
Sudermann, H., 5, 7; *Johannes*, 88.
Sullivan, J. L., his acting, 57.
Synge, J., 5.

Tarkington, B., 79.
Tellegen, L., romantic drama, 58.
Thomas, A., 5; *The Witching Hour*, 23; *The Copperhead*, 59.
Tolstoi, L., 5, 83; attack on Shakespeare, 95, 101, 102.
Towse, J. R., 134.
Tree, H. B., 47, 138.

Walker, S., his work as producer, 78, 79, 89.
Walter, E., 5; *The Heritage*, 59.
Wescott, H. D., founder of Yale Dramatic Association, 85.
Wheeler, A. C., remarks on scenic excess, 45.
Wilcox, E. W., play from Esther, 89.
Wilde, O., 5; *Salomé*, 88.
Williams, J., 5, 59.
Winter, W., his attacks on the theatre, 111–113.

Yeats, W. B., 5.

Ziegfeld, F., his letter on ticket-speculating, 48–51.